Picture This!

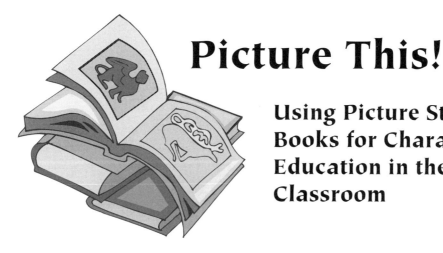

Picture This!

Using Picture Story Books for Character Education in the Classroom

Claire Gatrell Stephens

LIBRARIES

UNLIMITED

A Member of the Greenwood Publishing Group

Westport, Connecticut • London

British Library Cataloguing in Publication Data is available.

Copyright © 2004 by Claire Gatrell Stephens

ISBN: 1–59158–001–4

First published in 2004

Libraries Unlimited, 88 Post Road West, Westport, CT 06881
A Member of the Greenwood Publishing Group, Inc.
www.lu.com

Printed in the United States of America

The paper used in this book complies with the Permanent Paper Standard issued by the National Information Standards Organization (Z39.48–1984).

10   9   8   7   6   5   4   3   2

With thanks, praise and a prayer this book is offered to God in the hope that it will be used to accomplish great things in the lives of children.

For my sister, Julia Leigh Gatrell, who inspires us all with her passionate concern about the character of others.

Contents

Acknowledgments

Book Credits

American Too. Used by permission of HarperCollins Publishers. Text and illustrations copyright 1996.

Excerpt and Book Cover from *America's Champion Swimmer: Gertrude Ederle*, text copyright © 2000 by David A. Adler, illustration copyright © 2000 by Terry Widener, reproduced by permission of Harcourt, Inc.

Baseball Saved Us. Text copyright © 1993 by Ken Mochizuki. Illustrations copyright © 1993 by Dom Lee. Permission arranged with Lee & Low Books, Inc., NY, NY 10016.

Don't Need Friends by Carolyn Crimi, used with permission of Dragonfly Books, an imprint of Random House Children's Books, a division of Random House, Inc.

Enemy Pie by Derek Munson, illustrated by Tara Calahan King © 2000. Reprinted by permission of Chronicle Books, San Francisco.

The Flag We Love used with permission by Charlesbridge Publishing, Inc.

The Gift by Marcia A. Freeman courtesy of Maupin House, 2002. www.maupinhouse.com.

Hey Little Ant—Reproduced with permission from *Hey Little Ant*. Text copyright ©1998 by Phillip and Hannah Hoose. Art copyright ©1998 by Debbie Tilley. Tricycle Press, P.O. Box 7123 Berkeley, CA 94707. Available from your local bookseller or call 800-841-2665. Visit Tricycle on the web at www.tenspeed.com.

Hooway for Wodney Wat © 1999. Text by Helen Lester. Illustrations by Lynn Munsinger. Used by permission of Houghton Mifflin Company.

Just Plain Fancy by Patricia Polacco used with permission of Dell Yearling, an imprint of Random House Children's Books, a division of Random House, Inc.

Excerpt and Jacket Illustration from *Oliver Button Is a Sissy*, copyright © 1979 by Tomie dePaola, reprinted by permission of Harcourt, Inc.

Rocks in His Head, text copyright © 2001 by Carol Otis Hurst. Illustrations copyright © 2001 by James Stevenson. Used by permission of HarperCollins Publishers.

Excerpt and Jacket Illustration from *Smoky Night*, text copyright © 1994 by Eve Bunting. Jacket Illustration copyright © 1994 by David Diaz. Both are reprinted by permission of Harcourt, Inc.

Snail Started It! by Katja Reider. Illustrated by Angela von Roehl. Used by permission of Sea Star Books, a division of North-South Books.

This Land Is Your Land by Woody Guthrie. Copyright © 1998 by Kathy Jakobsen. Used by permission of Little, Brown and Company, (Inc.).

What's So Terrible about Swallowing an Apple Seed? Text copyright © 1996 by Harriet Lerner and Susan Goldhor. Illustrations copyright © 1996 by Catharine O'Neill. Used by permission of HarperCollins Publishers.

Photo Credits

David A. Adler photo courtesy of the author.

Eve Bunting photo courtesy of the author.

Carolyn Crimi photo courtesy of the author.

Tomie dePaola photo by Mario Mercado, courtesy of the author.

Marcia Freeman photo courtesy of Maupin House Publishers.

Woody Guthrie photo courtesy of the Woody Guthrie Foundation and Archives.

Philip and Hannah Hoose photo by David A. Rogers, courtesy of Tricycle Press, Berkeley, CA.

Carol Otis Hurst photo and biographical information courtesy of the author.

Patrice Kennedy photo courtesy of Maupin House Publishers.

Tara Calahan King photo and biography courtesy of the illustrator.

Harriet Lerner and Susan Goldhor photo courtesy of Worley Shoemaker Artist Management.

Helen Lester photo courtesy of Houghton Mifflin Co.

Ted Lewin photo used with permission of the illustrator.

Ralph Masiello photo courtesy of the illustrator.

Lynn Munsinger (*Don't Need Friends*), photo courtesy of the illustrator.

Lynn Munsinger (*Hooway for Wodney Wat*), photo courtesy of Houghton Mifflin Co.

Derek Munson photo and biography courtesy of the author.

Patricia Polacco photo by Kenn Klein, courtesy of the author.

Pam Muñoz Ryan photo courtesy of Charlesbridge Publishing.

Terry Widener photo courtesy of Michelle Manasse.

Graphic Credits

Clip art used by permission of Art Today/ClipArt.com.

KidSource graphic by Craig Stephens, used by permission.

Parent Zone graphic by Craig Stephens, used by permission.

TeachSource graphic by Craig Stephens, used by permission.

Pledge of Allegiance Coloring Page courtesy of Effective Promotions, Troy, New York.

Personal Acknowledgments

Susan A. Bobson MSW, LISW, Worthington, Ohio. For her wonderful picture book suggestions.

Sharon Coatney at Libraries Unlimited for connecting me with the idea for this book and shepherding me through its development.

Curriculum Materials Center, University of Central Florida, Orlando, Florida.

Educator's Resource Center, Orange County Public Schools, Orlando, Florida.

Gretchen English, Language Arts Teacher, Walker Middle School, Orlando, Florida.

Julie Gatrell, Guidance Department, Cherokee School, Orlando, Florida.

Lonnie Holt, Media Clerk, Walker Middle School, Orlando, Florida.

Joan LaBoy, Guidance Department Chair, Walker Middle School, Orlando, Florida.

Lois Lippitt, Library Volunteer, Walker Middle School, Orlando, Florida.

Debby Mattil for her encouragement.

Orange County Library System, Orlando, Florida.

Cheryl Pope, Language Arts Department Chair, Walker Middle School, Orlando, Florida.

Pattie Smith, Media Specialist, University High School, Orange County Public Schools, Orlando, Florida.

Craig Stephens, husband extraordinaire!

Amy Torres, Teacher of the Gifted, Walker Middle School, Orlando, Florida.

Word Weavers Writer's Critique Group, Orlando, Florida.

Part I

An Introduction
to Character
Education

An Introduction to Character Education

As I finished work on this project, it happened again. In Red Lion, Pennsylvania, a fourteen-year-old boy walked into his junior high school cafeteria armed with a 44-caliber Magnum that he took from a safe in his home. He shot the school principal in the chest, killing him. The boy then turned the gun on himself, taking his own life with a shot to the head. Thankfully, these dramatic events do not happen every day. Yet they do happen with sufficient frequency that we seem to be increasingly less alarmed by them. Do we really want to develop a societal attitude that shrugs off these occurrences as "just another school shooting"?

Far from being another "add-on," character education is rapidly earning a place in the required core curriculum of school districts across the United States. Recognizing the mixed messages students receive from television and movies, the many social problems students face from various sources, and the many problems associated with the breakdown of the family, educators are seeking ways to teach core values that were once taught exclusively in the home. In her article "Character Education by the Book," Claudia Logan (2003) quotes Eleanor Childes, founder of the Heartwood Institute, a nonprofit ethics program. Childes made the following observation about the need for character education:

At first I blamed TV, which does play a part in some of the violence we see. I blamed drugs and the breakdown of the family, but then I began to think a lot about culture and about how so much of our understanding of character comes from stories. . . . We have exposed our children to violent images without the guidance and nurturing needed to help them make hard decision and choices. Children have big hearts if developed with care, they must be helped to understand that the mind must work along with the heart—that they need to think before acting. This impulsive acting, by the way, is not limited to inner-city youth. We must all gather our children around the campfire.

By virtue of their age, children lack the skills for solid character judgment. Researches including Jean Piaget, William Damon, and Robert Selman have studied the moral development of children. The consensus of their work, and the work of others, is that children respond to moral issues in a way that is tied to their ability to reason. This information takes on further importance when we recognize that our classrooms are no longer homogeneous collections of students who come to school with similar backgrounds and experiences. Twenty-first-century schools reflect a diversity of community that was virtually nonexistent fifty years ago. Our students' ability to think and reason is as varied as their backgrounds. We must assess their needs and meet them at the stage of development that they have reached. This is true for their academic needs as well as their social development, hence the need for character development in the classroom. In their book *Literature-Based Moral Education,* authors Lamme, Krogh, and Yachmetz (1992, p. 10) point out that "Children grow more and internalize their moral beliefs when they have opportunities to reason and think things through at their own level. We adults must stifle our efforts to preach about morals and instead learn to facilitate children's own thinking about these issues." Quality literature provides an excellent resource to gather our children around the campfire and meet this need. Good stories provide students with neutral ground where they can comfortably confront problems and choices. Stories provide access to different cultures, experiences, and attitudes, challenging students to think and evaluate the world around them. It is from this critical thinking that their moral compass will develop.

This book is not intended to be a character education program. (For readers interested in developing such a program, I provide a list of resources at the end of the Introduction.) This book should be used to supplement whatever character education curriculum your school or district has already adopted. Teachers using this book should carefully read and consider the ideas and exercises presented. Make careful decisions about classroom implementation based on your students, school, and community. Consider the standards, benchmarks, goals, and objectives put in place by your curriculum guidelines and select only those activities and exercises that are best suited to your students and your school community.

I hope you will enjoy the books and the activities you choose to do with your students. It is also my hope that you will find yourself personally challenged as you work with your character education curriculum. After all, being a person of character is not something that just happens. Positive character is a matter of daily choices made throughout our lives. Recognizing our own character challenges will help us be better teachers and to model positive examples for our students . Perhaps the best lesson we can give our children is to help them understand there is no one-time "quick fix" to being a good person. Teaching and learning lessons in character help to arm both teacher and student for the complex challenges we face in our world today. Character education may have started as a trendy "add-on" several years ago, but its place in our curriculum has become essential.

To return to Eleanor Childes's analogy, it is time to gather our children, and ourselves, around the campfire. It is time to think, and talk, and reason. It is time to think about the type of society in which we want our children to live as adults. It is time for us as their teachers, parents, and leaders to challenge them at their level so that they grow into quality adults who will lead their own children to good character.

Tips for Teaching and Handling Character Education in the Classroom

As you begin working with a character education curriculum, you may want to incorporate some of these ideas:

- You are an example. Practice what you preach. As teachers, we are role models at school and in the community. It is important to remember this at all times.
- Establish a clear curriculum and a set of goals with which you can personally identify.

- Establish a safe classroom environment so that students know everyone will treat them respectfully during activities and class discussions.

- Spend time building a common vocabulary in the classroom. Do not assume all children attach the same meaning to terms such as courage, love, and so on. Identify those attributes with which you plan to work in your curriculum and build a common base for classroom discussion.

- Plan ahead—be organized to keep lessons, projects, and activities flowing in a timely manner so that students associate the stories, books, exercises, and activities to the common theme.

- Use visual aids such as charts or Venn diagrams during class discussions to help build connections and incorporate different learning styles.

- Link ideas and concepts to everyday life and experiences in and out of the classroom.

- Let conversation flow, accepting all ideas that come up. Role model respectful ways to express disagreement.

- Revisit books and values as needed throughout the year.

- Students should not be forced to share. They should share only if they are comfortable and feel the need to contribute to the values conversation.

- Allow for individual reflection through journal writing, drawing pictures, and so on. If necessary, students can conference privately with the instructor about their thoughts and feelings.

- Partner or small-group work (writing, discussion, sharing, projects, etc.) can be helpful. Plan your groups carefully and construct assignments so that all students must participate.

- Provide opportunities for students to demonstrate good character by participating in activities related to the topic. Community service projects can be established for a variety of needs and organized by the students. These projects can benefit the classroom, school, or community at large.

- Recognize students for demonstrating outstanding character. This recognition can be for participation in class activities and projects. You should also recognize random acts of good character you observe outside of official class activities. Students need to know that their character is on display on the playground, in the lunchroom, at home, and so on. Doing this can involve formal recognition with certificates and awards but also can include a quiet word of specific praise in response to an observed action.

Tips for Including Parents and Community Members in Your Character Education Curriculum

Open communication is important to ensuring that no parent or community group feels your curriculum will infringe on their beliefs, values, or culture. To increase communication, try these ideas:

- Create a regular newsletter to let parents and community members know what is happening in the classroom.

- Recommend books for families to read to their children. Provide discussion questions to go with the books.

- Invite parents and community members to the classroom to read books and share their own stories.

- Seek out guest speakers to visit with the class and discuss experiences related to the character trait under discussion.

- Plan family night events where students and family members can interact with each other on activities related to the character education curriculum.

- Seek out ways that students can share their knowledge by participating in community events, festivals, and groups.

- Network with local public libraries and other organizations to create a communitywide emphasis on character traits as they are taught.

Classroom Management and Character Education

Despite our best efforts, things sometimes go awry. The following tips may help resolve classroom disruption problems that occur during character education lessons.

For General Problems

- Assess the situation so you don't overreact; you do not want to make a tactless or thoughtless child feel they have done something irrevocable. Watch for repeat behavior.
- Remember it is the behavior exhibited by the child that is the problem. Try to keep the focus on the behavior so that you do not personally attack the child.

When Someone Says or Does Something Rude, Insulting, or Prejudicial

- Evaluate the situation; can you deal with the remark immediately in front of the class, or should you address the offending student in private? Be sure that you do not demean the offending student as you address the situation.
- Politely ask the student on what experience or facts he or she is basing the opinion. Educate the student to help him or her consider other points of view.
- Try to build empathy. Ask the student to imagine that someone who might be hurt by the remark is sitting in on the discussion. Would the student still make the offending remark? How would the student feel if someone said something offensive to or about him or her?
- If the comments persist, tell the student such remarks are inappropriate for school. Follow your school's guidelines to involve a guidance counselor and parent(s) (or caregivers) in a conference. Meet separately with the parent or parents; assure them you are an advocate for their child. If possible, establish a plan to help the student learn about correct behavior. Establish a relationship with an adult or older student mentor to help the student. Establish reasonable consequences for the offending behavior and follow through with them if necessary.
- Contact the wronged student's parent or caregiver. Explain what happened. Assure the parent that the situation is being addressed, and urge him or her not to overreact. Consult with your school's administration and guidance staff. If possible, involve the wronged student's parents in resolving the situation.

Character Education Resources

Those seeking information on character education curricula should carefully research the options available, seeking the best match for your students, school, and community. Be sure to carefully study the organization; ask to see credentials, check for hidden agendas, and verify research claims. A simple Internet search will yield countless groups and organizations offering complete curriculum packages or individual lesson plans. Although I am not endorsing any particular group or organization, the following sources provide a starting point for any search and reveal the variety of materials available.

Center for Civic Education, 5146 Douglas Fir Road, Calabasas, CA 91302-1467. (818) 591-9321. Available: http://www.civiced.org/.

CHARACTER COUNTS! National Office, Josephson Institute of Ethics, 4640 Admiralty Way, Suite 1001, Marina del Rey, CA 90292-6610. (310) 306-1868. Available: http://www. charactercounts.org.

Character Education Center, P.O. Box 80208, R.S.M., CA 92688-0208. (800) 229-3455. Available: http://allaboutrespect.net/.

The Character Education Partnership, 1025 Connecticut Avenue NW, Suite 1011, Washington, DC 20036. (800) 988-8081. Available: http://www.character.org/.

Characterplus™ (a project of the Cooperating School Districts), 8225 Florissant Road, St. Louis, MO 63121. (800) 835-8282. Available: http://csd.org/staffdev/chared/characterplus.html.

The Heartwood Institute, 425 North Craig Street, Suite 302, Pittsburgh, PA 15213. (800) 432-7810. Available: http://www.heartwoodethics.org/.

National Center for Youth Issues, (Home of STARS—Students Taking a Right Stand), P.O. Box 22185, Chattanooga, TN 37422-2185. (800) 477-8277. Available: http://www.ncyi.org/.

References

Lamme, Linda Leonard, Suzanne Lowell Krogh, and Kathy A. Yachmetz. *Literature-Based Moral Education: Children's Books and Activities for Teaching Values, Responsibility, and Good Judgment in the Elementary School.* Phoenix, Arizona: Oryx Press, 1992.

Logan, Claudia. "Character Education by the Book." Available online at Scholastic.com: http:// teacher.scholastic.com/professional/todayschild/charatered.htm. Accessed March 19, 2003.

Part II

The Books and Lessons

1

Citizenship and Patriotism

*And so, my fellow Americans: ask not what your country can do for you—
ask what you can do for your country.*

John F. Kennedy (1917–1963)
Inaugural Address
January 20, 1961

In post–September 11 America, patriotism has taken on new meaning. We are rediscovering a sense of national pride and heritage that had been dormant for a long time. These books provide us with three perspectives on citizenship and patriotism. *American Too* focuses on the immigrant experience by exploring what being American means to one young girl. Our flag, an important national symbol, is the focus of *The Flag We Love*. Finally, *This Land Is Your Land* uses an important cultural icon, Woody Guthrie's well-known folk song, to focus our attention on being a citizen in our democratic society. These books will help you and your students explore the American experience. You will come away enriched in your knowledge of this great country and with an increased pride in your role as an American citizen.

American Too by Elisa Bartone

Rosie ran down the stairs and out of the building. . . . All she could think was, "How can I show everyone I'm really American?"

Bartone, Elisa. *American Too*. Illustrated by Ted Lewin. New York: Lothrop, Lee & Shepard Books, 1996. ISBN 0-688-13278-2.

Reading Level: 5.5

Interest Level: K–3 (Higher if tied in thematically with instruction)

The Story

Based on a true family story, *American Too* is an inspiring tale of heritage and new beginnings. When Rosina and her family arrive in New York, her mother tells her that anything is possible in America. As she admires the Statue of Liberty from the deck of their ship, Rosina believes this is true. Rosina longs to be a modern American girl. She changes her name to Rosie and begins to reject things that reflect her Italian heritage. When her father tells Rosie she will be queen of the feast of San Gennaro, Rosie rebels. As she walks the streets of New York, Rosie is inspired. She knows how to be both queen of the feast and show her American pride.

The people in her neighborhood prepare for the feast while Rosie makes preparations of her own. On the day of the feast, she enjoys all the festivities. When the time comes for the queen to join in the parade, Rosie joins the group in a Statue of Liberty costume. With the support of the cheering crowd, she proudly leads the parade carrying her torch high. As the story ends, Rosie realizes that it is good for her and her family to remember their heritage even as they become modern Americans.

Character Connections

Rosie's story mirrors the experiences of many immigrants. Her quest to be a modern American girl is really a search for what it means to be American. Ultimately, Rosie learns that being American is about being a good citizen, which, for Rosie, means being an Italian American. It also means displaying pride and patriotism for her new home. Rosie learns that good citizens can do both. *American Too* offers readers a chance to consider their citizenship in this great land in the context of the diversity of its people. It provides a great opportunity to introduce the "melting pot" concept of American society and to look at ways in which we live together. Students can learn about the importance of citizenship by learning about, respecting, and embracing the many diverse cultures that make up modern American life, just as Rosie learned she could embrace her native cultural identity and her newfound American pride.

About the Author

Elisa Bartone teaches in the New York City Public Schools and resides on Staten Island. She earned a master's degree in elementary education. She has written several children's books, including a Caldecott honor book, *Pepe the Lamplighter*, also illustrated by Ted Lewin. *American Too* was inspired by a true story told to Bartone by her great-uncle.

About the Illustrator

Ted Lewin is a talented artist who, even as a child growing up in Buffalo, New York, wanted to be an illustrator. He was the only one in his family who could draw, and he was always encouraged to develop his talents. He attended the prestigious Pratt Institute to study art, where he met his wife, Jane, also an artist and illustrator. The Lewins enjoy an active life that includes traveling and other outdoor activities. Often their trips inspire books, such as *Faithful Elephant*, which Lewin created after their first trip to Africa. Students may find it interesting to know that Lewin worked as a professional wrestler to earn the money needed for art school. This story is told in his memoir *I Was a Teenage Professional Wrestler*, which was an American Library Association (ALA) Notable Book in 1993. Lewin has authored more than ten books and illustrated many more for other authors.

Objectives

After reading this book, students will be able to

- Define related vocabulary.
- Demonstrate understanding of the story by answering related questions.
- Discuss and define the meaning of citizenship and identify examples of good citizenship.
- Demonstrate citizenship by identifying ways to contribute to the school community and participating in at least one citizenship activity.

Classroom Exercises

Prereading Activity

Discuss the word *immigrate*. Identify reasons someone might want to leave his or her own country and move to the United States. Ask students what they think happens to people when they leave their country and move to a new land. Do the people forget their native land and its customs? Do they immediately become just like all the people in their new home? After a brief discussion, introduce the story by telling students it is about a girl who left Italy and came to the United States.

Vocabulary

Students may need help defining the following terms. Define the terms either before reading the story or, using context clues while reading, after you have finished. Note: *American Too* contains several Italian phrases that are explained in the text, so they are not listed here. Depending on your students, you may wish to include them in a vocabulary study for this book.

superstitious	Rudolph Valentino	mass
evil eye	gesture	bocce
biscotti	modern	procession
gawk, gawking	crescent moon	shrine

Comprehension and Values Questions

Select and use only those questions suited for your class or group. Some questions ask about story facts, but others require the students to analyze story events. Higher-level questions may bring a variety of answers; ask students to justify their response with examples from the story to support their point.

- What did Rosina's mother tell her about living in America?
- Why did the girls make fun of Rosina? How did Rosina respond to the girls? How do you think Rosina felt when the girls teased her?
- What did Rosina want to be?
- Name at least two things Rosina did to try to make herself into a modern American girl.
- Identify things in the story that show Italian culture.
- What did Papa tell Rosie about the Feast of San Gennaro?
- How did Rosie react to the news that she would be queen?
- Describe two ways the people prepared for the feast.
- Describe two things that happened on the feast day.
- What surprise did Rosie reveal when she appeared as queen? How did the crowd react? Why do you think they reacted the way they did?
- Who asked Rosie to dance? How was he dressed?
- Rosie could have refused to be the queen of the feast. Why do you think Rosie participated? What lesson do you think Rosie learned by being a part of the feast?

Character Exercises

Purchase or create enough bags of multicolored jellybeans to accommodate your class when divided into small groups of four to five students. You will also need paper cups or small plastic bowls and larger plastic bags to remix the candy. Before starting, have students wash their hands and give each group clean paper towels to cover their desktops. Give each group a bag of jellybeans and enough cups or bowls to divide the candy up by colors. After the bags are divided, collect each color in a larger plastic bag, and give each group one of the colors. Tell the students those are their jellybeans to eat; they cannot have another color. Students may not like the color they have been given, or they may wish to have more than one color. Use this as the starting point for a class discussion using some of the following questions as prompts:

- Is it okay with you to have only one color of jellybean to eat? Why or why not?
- Why might it be better to have a variety of jellybean colors to eat?
- Do you think a bag of jellybeans is best with only one color or with many colors? Why? Explain.
- How is this bag of jellybeans like our country? Do you see any similarities between the jellybeans and the American people?

Guide the discussion to help students see the advantage of having a multicolored bag with lots of flavors and colors from which to choose. As you begin to make comparisons between the jellybeans and America, walk around the room with a large plastic bag; remix all the individual colors together in the bag. Explain that America is like a bag of jellybeans. People from many different cultures and lands come to America bringing their unique heritage with them. Each group contributes to America and helps to make our country a better place to live. When all the candies are back in the large bag, be sure they are well mixed; distribute them for students to eat.

Refer to the *Integrate Your Curriculum* section for additional ideas that explore cultural contributions and citizenship.

Integrate Your Curriculum

Art

- Ask students to draw a picture of a community or cultural event celebrated in their family or community. Use the pictures to create a bulletin board display for the school or class. Be sure to allow students to explain their pictures so everyone in the class learns about the various events.

Language Arts

- Possible journal topics:
  - Ask students to write a paragraph or short paper explaining the picture they drew showing the community or cultural event celebrated by their family. Students might explain the event, its history, how they celebrate, and so on.
  - Identify some superstitions and explain what they are.
  - Even though Rosie thought the Feast of San Gennaro was "old-fashioned" and Italian, she seemed to enjoy it. What do you think this showed about her?
  - Why do you think Rosie wanted so much to be modern?
  - Write a paragraph comparing what Rosina and her brother ate for breakfast with a typical American breakfast. Ask students to tell which they think is better and why.
  - Ask students to identify some of characteristics of Italian culture shown in the story and then list a comparable number of characteristics of American culture. Students can then write a paragraph comparing and contrasting the two.
  - Ask students to imagine they moved to Italy. Ask them to list and explain three things they would have to do to be able to feel like they belonged in their new country.

Physical Education

- Arrange for a demonstration or learn how to play Bocce and set up a class tournament.

Social Studies

- For enrichment, hold a culture day in your classroom. Invite parents and community members to participate. Include representatives from each of the cultural groups represented in your class. Include games, clothing, foods, music, language, clothing, and so on. This event will allow students the chance to learn about different cultures and to realize how various groups have contributed to American culture.

- Identify elements of good citizenship displayed by the people in the story such as helping with the festival, enjoying the game of bocce (good sportsmanship), displaying patriotism by cheering Rosie's Statue of Liberty costume, and so on. Contrast this with elements of bad citizenship shown in the story such as the girls teasing Rosie or her angry outburst when Papa told Rosie she would be queen. Use the worksheet included in this section to allow students to explore and define the concept of good citizenship.

• Locate Italy on a map and study the country.

• Find someone who speaks Italian in your community. Invite them to visit the class and teach the students how to say and write several phrases in Italian.

• Look up information on San Gennaro. Who was this saint? Why is his feast day important? Is it still celebrated in Italy today?

• Study the Statue of Liberty and Uncle Sam. What is the history of these American symbols? Ask students to write a paragraph explaining what they mean to them.

PARENTZONE: TAKING THE LESSON HOME

Rosie ultimately displays good citizenship in the story by contributing to the community celebration as queen and by participating in all the festival's events and activities. Collaborate with parents and community members to compile a list of events scheduled in your area during the coming weeks. These events can be communitywide celebrations or smaller local events at school, at church, or in a neighborhood, for example. Include on the list event dates, times, and locations. If possible, include a contact person and phone number for someone coordinating each event. Encourage parents to take their children to at least one of the events and, if possible, volunteer some time as a family to help the event staff.

TEACHSOURCE: RESOURCES FOR TEACHERS

Januarius is an online resource about Saint Gennaro, available: http://www.catholic-forum.com/ saints/saintj30.htm.

Ted Lewin, the official Web site of the illustrator. Available: http://www.tedlewin.com.

Time for Citizenship.Com is an interactive Web site featuring lesson plans, activities, and more for teachers, students, and parents. Available: http://www.timeforcitizenship.com/default/index.asp?t=welcome.

KIDSSOURCE: RESOURCES FOR STUDENTS

Di Franco, J. Phillip. *The Italian Americans.* The Immigrant Experience series. New York: Chelsea House, 1996. ISBN 0-7910-3353-8. Not for primary grades, this book provides good background on Italian American life and history in the United States.

Raatma, Lucia. *Patriotism.* Character Education series. Mankato, MN: Bridgestone Books, 2000. ISBN 0-7368-0509-5.

Symbols and Celebrations—American FAQs. Available: http://www.usia.gov/usa/usa.htm/facts/symbols.htm.

American Too: **Good Citizenship**

Do this exercise in small groups of three or four students. Be prepared to share your answers with the class.

Rosie demonstrated good citizenship in American Too by obeying her father, even though she did not want to at first. By participating in the festival, she was able to honor her Italian heritage and show her American patriotism. In your group, do some brainstorming; how can we be good citizens each day?

Acts that show good citizenship:

1. _____

2. _____

3. _____

4. _____

5. _____

Share your examples with the class and listen to the examples of other groups. Then work with your group again to define citizenship. Share and discuss your definition with the class. After hearing all the definitions, work with your teacher and classmates to create a class definition of good citizenship.

Good citizenship is _____

_____

_____

_____

Finally finish the following sentence and share your response with the class:

I will demonstrate good citizenship by _____.

American Too: Demonstrating Citizenship

Rosie demonstrated good citizenship by serving as queen of the festival. Sometimes we serve our community in ways that are not as exciting. We might serve by picking up trash or weeding a flowerbed, for example.

Your teacher will arrange for you to walk around your school. In the spaces below, list things you see that need improvement. Some examples might be straightening up the library, cleaning out a storage room, updating a bulletin board, or removing litter from the playground.

Possible school improvement ideas:

1. _____

2. _____

3. _____

Share your examples with the class. Create a list of all the ideas, then vote on one project for the entire class to do together. In the space below, brainstorm how you will complete the project. Then share these ideas with your class and develop a plan to demonstrate your good citizenship at school.

Our class citizenship project is _____ .

Materials needed:	Steps to accomplish:	Responsible person:

Planning our service project:

The Flag We Love by Pam Muñoz Ryan

A citizen wears a symbol
A tiny, flag-shaped pin
As a promise for our future
and a reminder of where we've been.

Ryan, Pam Muñoz. *The Flag We Love*. Illustrated by Ralph Masiello. Watertown, MA: Charlesbridge, 2000. ISBN 0-88106-845-4.

Reading Level: 5.5

Interest Level: 5–8 (All grades if tied in thematically with instruction)

The Story

An inspirational tribute to Old Glory, *The Flag We Love* contains something for everyone. Using patriotic verse and historical facts, the book explores how the Stars and Stripes became an enduring American symbol. Readers will gain an appreciation of the flag's meaning and insights into its place in our heritage and culture. Whether an established American citizen or new to our shores, readers are sure to learn something from this picture book. In addition, pride in our nation, its flag, and its history will increase tenfold as students join with others in celebrating *The Flag We Love*.

Character Connections

The book celebrates old-fashioned American patriotism. Students studying its text will gain understanding of why we pledge to the flag, where and how the flag is displayed, and what the flag means to the citizens of this country. This knowledge will lead students to an increased understanding of the value attached to their citizenship in this great land and serves as a starting point for studying American culture, heritage, and values.

About the Author

Pam Muñoz Ryan lives in Leucadia, California, with her family. She grew up in the San Joaquin Valley where she discovered the library. She often went there to escape the one-hundred-degree–plus summer temperatures. Inside its air-conditioned walls, she became hooked on reading. She discovered that a good book could take her anywhere she wanted to go and let her become anything she wanted to be.

Ryan has written many books for children, including *Amelia and Eleanor Go for a Ride,* an ALA Notable Book, and *Esperanza Rising,* based on the life of her grandmother, which was selected as one of the top ten books for young adults by the ALA in 2001.

About the Illustrator

The father of two daughters, Ralph Masiello lives in Worcester, Massachusetts. He is a graduate of the Rhode Island School of Design and creates works displayed and sold in fine art galleries in addition to illustrating children's books. His oil paintings are rich in color and remarkably realistic. Masiello's art breathes life into the subjects of his books. In fact, children have affectionately nicknamed him "The Icky Bug Man" because of the power of his artwork. The name comes from the title of two of the books he illustrated *The Icky Bug Alphabet Book* and *The Icky Bug Counting Book.*

Objectives

After reading this book, students will be able to

• Identify five facts about the flag.

• Explain what the flag means to them.

Classroom Exercises

Prereading Activity

Give students time to complete the flag-coloring page included in this section. Then ask the students to stand in the class and recite the pledge to the flag as a group. Ask them if they know why we pledge to the flag. You might also ask what the pledge means or what the design of our flag represents. Use the overhead or chalkboard to brainstorm a list of "want to know" questions about the flag based on your discussion. Return to the list after reading the book to ensure that all the questions are answered.

Vocabulary

Students may need help defining the following terms. Define the terms either before reading the story or, using context clues while reading, after you have finished.

symbol	Stars and Stripes
connotation	allegiance
intention	e pluribus unum
banner	

Comprehension and Values Questions

Because *The Flag We Love* is not a story in the usual sense, try this exploration activity. Divide students into small groups; give each group a copy of the book. Assign students one or more of the following points for discussion. After a brief time for discussion, groups should report their findings to the entire class.

- List all the patriotic customs you can find for displaying the flag.
- List as many people as you can who have had an impact on the history of our flag. Briefly explain what each person did.
- List as many places as you can where the flag is flown. What is the most faraway place the flag has flown?
- List as many ways as you can that people use the flag to express their patriotism, their citizenship, rights of citizenship, or their feelings.
- List as many things as you can that our flag represents.
- Conclude this discussion by asking students to list five things that they learned about the flag and explain or describe what the flag means to them personally.

Character Exercises

- As an act of community service, involve the class in taking care of the school flag for a month. Teach them how to raise and lower the flag, fold and store it properly. Once your class has learned how to care for the flag, enlist another teacher to allow your class to share their knowledge with his or her students. The new teacher's class could then take over caring for the flag and pass it on to another class.
- If your school produces its own news program, ask if your class can lead the Pledge of Allegiance. This could be done live or on tape, as a group or by individuals.
- Form a color guard and practice presenting the colors. Consult with a local ROTC (Reserve Officers Training Corps), military, or scouting group for advice. Once your students have mastered the appropriate skills, have them present the colors and lead the pledge for assemblies, parent night events, or school programs such as concerts or plays.

Integrate Your Curriculum

Art

- After creating their own flag poem (see the Language Arts section), students can create an original illustration for their work. Combine the completed poems with their illustrations in a class flag book or use them to decorate a bulletin board.

Language Arts

- Have students create their own poems about the flag. Write an acrostic poem using words such as flag, freedom, patriotism, or another word of their choice. They can create a tribute poem to the flag or someone involved in the flag's history, such as Betsy Ross or Francis Hopkinson. Once written, the poems can be illustrated and then bound into a class book or displayed on a bulletin board.

Mathematics

- Subtraction Practice: Instruct students to go through the text identifying important dates and events in the text. Direct students to determine how long ago these events took place.

Social Studies

- Do a more in-depth study of some things mentioned in the book. Students can do this as a group project and bring their findings back to the class in the form of an oral report. Possible topics include how the flag has changed over the years, the pledge to the flag, correct uses of the flag, controversies involving the flag, flag myths, the meaning of the flag colors, display of the flag, and so on.

Laminate one of the students' flag drawings from this unit. Send it home with students, along with a note requesting parents to display it in a window where it will be visible to the outside world. Urge parents to display the flag as a symbol of the family's citizenship and patriotism.

Independence Hall Association. *The Betsy Ross Homepage*: Available: http://www.ushistory.org/betsy/. This is a great site for information about Betsy Ross and the history of our flag. It also features many good links to other related sites.

Miami-Dade County Public Schools. *Patriotism.Org.* Available: http://www.patriotism.org/index.html. This site, sponsored by the Miami-Dade County (Florida) school system, contains links to many patriotic holidays including Flag Day. Links to lesson plans offer additional ideas for studying our nation's flag.

National Flag Foundation. *Flags of America*. New York: Carousel Film and Video, 1992. This ten-minute video gives an overview of flag history.

Sedeen, Margaret. *Star-Spangled Banner: Our Nation and Its Flag*. Washington, DC: National Geographic Society, 1993. ISBN 0-87044-944-3. This book is full of pictures and photos documenting the history of the flag.

Streufert, Duane. *The Flag of the United States.* Available: http://www.usflag.org/toc.html. An excellent resource about the flag, this site contains information about history, etiquette, folding, flying, and so on. This Web site is best suited for upper elementary students and older. Lower grades will require help reading this site.

KIDSSOURCE: RESOURCES FOR STUDENTS

Ayer, Eleanor. *Our Flag.* I Know America series. Brookfield, CT: Millbrook Press, 1992. ISBN 1-56294-107-0.

Johnson, Linda Carlson. *Our National Symbols.* I Know America series. Brookfield, CT: Millbrook Press, 1992. ISBN 1-56294-108-9.

Did you know the Pledge of Allegiance was first recited in schools in 1892? It is an oath to our flag and our country.

The Pledge of Allegiance

I pledge allegiance to the flag of the United States of America
And to the republic for which it stands;
One nation under god, indivisible,
With liberty and justice for all.

I learned about our flag!

List five things you learned about our flag by reading The Flag We Love. Then color the flag picture above.

1. _____

2. _____

3. _____

4. _____

5. _____

What the Flag Means to Me

This Land Is Your Land by Woody Guthrie

And all around me a voice was sounding:
This land was made for you and me.

Guthrie, Woody. *This Land Is Your Land*. Illustrated by Kathy Jakobsen. New York: Little, Brown and Company, 1998. ISBN 0-15-269954-6.

Reading Level: 2.8

Interest Level: K–3 (All grades if tied in thematically with instruction)

The Story

Woody Guthrie's famous American folk ballad is beautifully illustrated in this book by artist Kathy Jakobsen. The book also includes a tribute by Pete Seeger, who provides some background on the song's history. A brief scrapbook section by author Janelle Yates provides biography information about the famous singer. A first-rate introduction to this classic song, its creator, and the times that inspired it, this book will educate, inform, and inspire readers of all ages.

Character Connections

Woody Guthrie's popular folk song celebrates America—at both her best and worst. The song was a triumph, becoming popular among people of all classes, cultures, and races. It remains instantly recognizable even now, more than fifty years after its first performance. "This land is your land. This land is my land. This land is made for you and me." These are simple ideas that cut to the heart of the American experience and express what our nation is about. America is a country that does not belong to the rich or to the people in charge, but to all of its citizens. Use *This Land Is Your Land* to focus on the civics of citizenship. How do we demonstrate civic responsibility? How do we as Americans demonstrate our ownership of this land? Kathy Jakobsen's beautiful illustrations for the last two verses of the song provide one visual interpretation of this. See how many more ideas you and your students can find.

About the Author

Woodrow Wilson Guthrie was born in Oklahoma during the summer of 1912. His early years were marked by tragedy, including the death of his sister in a fire and the serious illness of his mother. He learned to play the guitar at age seventeen. Woody found he enjoyed singing ballads and began writing songs that told of his experiences and the people he met.

During the Depression and Dust Bowl years, he moved west to California, where he found a job playing and singing on the radio. He went to New York in 1940, where he began to record some of his songs, including *This Land Is Your Land*. It was also during this time he met many of his lifelong friends, such as fellow musicians Pete Seeger and Leadbelly. Much of Woody Guthrie's fame was the result of his willingness to champion people of all colors and races, especially the poor. He died of Huntington's disease in 1967, but his message lives on in his books and music especially *This Land Is Your Land.*

About the Illustrator

The perfect choice to illustrate Woody Guthrie's ballad, Kathy Jakobsen is well known throughout the United States for her folk art. Her work is part of the permanent collections of the Smithsonian Institution and the Museum of American Folk Art. Well known for her oil paintings, Jakobsen is also a rising star in children's book illustration. She puts at least at least two thousand hours of painting time into each book she illustrates.

Objectives

After reading this book, students will be able to

- Define related vocabulary.

- State in their own words what the song means to them.

- Identify characteristics of good citizens.

- List how they can be responsible citizens at school and in their community.

Classroom Exercises

Prereading Activity

Locate and play a recording of *This Land Is Your Land* for the students. Encourage a class sing-along during the chorus. Ask students what they know about the song and what it means to them. Allow several students to comment, then turn the focus to the book and read it together.

Vocabulary

Students may need help defining the following terms. Define the words before reading or, using context clues while reading, when you are done.

redwood	trespassing
Gulf Stream	relief office
Dust Bowl (dust clouds)	Depression

Comprehension and Values Questions

Select and use only those questions that are suited for your class or group. Some questions ask about story facts, but others require the students to analyze story events. Higher-level questions may bring a variety of answers; ask students to justify their response with examples from the story to support their point.

- What does Woody Guthrie mean by "the New York island"?
- Where are the redwood forests? Where is the Gulf Stream?
- What do you think Woody Guthrie meant when he wrote the line, "This land was made for you and me"? How can America be your land and my land?
- Read the verse again that tells about the "No Trespassing" sign and the relief office. What do you think Woody Guthrie is trying to say in these lines?
- Why do you think this song has remained so popular?

Character Exercises

- Locate a jigsaw puzzle of the United States. Divide the pieces among your students and then challenge them to put the puzzle together. When finished, point out that they made America and that they make America.
- Assist students in learning the word *democracy* and defining it. Brainstorm a list of ways citizens in a democracy demonstrate good citizenship. Your list might include the following:
  - Staying informed about important community concerns and events.
  - In a positive way, participating in discussions and debates about important issues.
  - Recognizing the rights of individuals to differences of opinion and belief.
  - Voting in elections and referendums.
  - Obeying laws and rules.
  - Respecting authority.
  - Participating in community events.
  - Treating all people with respect and dignity.

Depending on your class, your list will vary and may contain characteristics not listed here.

- Because they are young, students may feel it is difficult to act as responsible citizens. Be sure to point out that, for example, even though they cannot vote, students can still participate in elections by helping with a campaign or staying informed about candidates and issues. Urge students to think creatively about ways to be good citizens. Using the worksheet included with this chapter, ask students to explain democracy in their own words and to list ways that they can be good citizens in the United States.
- As a culminating activity, make a good citizenship chain. Cut different colors of construction paper into strips. Ask the students to write a quality of good citizenship on their strip, then use glue or tape to connect the ends of the strips, linking them together to form a chain. Be sure to point out to the students that the chain is like our country. Each link represents them as citizens of the country and that we all must work together to make our country a good place to live.

Integrate Your Curriculum

Art

- Study folk art as a style or genre of art. Identify its characteristics, elements, and history. Encourage students to draw their own folk art pictures depicting the song and showing their neighborhood or community. Scan the pictures and create a PowerPoint slide show. Locate and secure the rights to use a recorded copy of *This Land Is Your Land* as background accompaniment. If a multimedia presentation is not possible, use the pictures to decorate a hallway in your school.

Music

- Work with your music teacher to learn and perform the song. Students might present the song at an assembly or a parent night along with the national anthem.

Science

- The following are mentioned in the song and could be investigated from a scientific point of view: Redwood trees, the Gulf Stream, deserts, wheat, dust storms, and the Dust Bowl.
- Woody Guthrie died from Huntington's disease. Investigate this illness to find out about its causes, treatments, and research for a cure.

Social Studies

- Learn about the Great Depression focusing on its effects on people. This can be tied in with a study of Woody Guthrie's life and travels. Students should be able to identify the era in terms of events, its effects on people, and its place in time.
- Study Woody Guthrie as a man and creative artist. Learn about his childhood, politics, songs, and books. Discuss the history of *This Land Is Your Land* in context of the history presented in Pete Seeger's tribute. Does learning about the author and his beliefs affect your feelings about the song?
- Explore the geographic terms used in the song to be sure students understand their meaning. These terms include *valley, desert,* and *island.*

Language Arts

- As an exercise in poetry, encourage students to write their own verses to the song, reflecting their neighborhood and community.
- Ask students to write a journal entry explaining what they think the song means and how America can belong to all of us.

PARENTZONE: TAKING THE LESSON HOME

Send students home with a piece of drawing or construction paper. Ask parents to sit with their children and either create a civic responsibility collage or create a drawing that shows an act of good citizenship. The collages or drawings might show someone voting, recycling, respecting the law, or assisting in a community project, for example. Urge parents to talk with their children while they do this project together, discussing what good citizenship means. Finally, students should return their drawings to class for presentation and discussion.

TEACHSOURCE: RESOURCES FOR TEACHERS

Catastrophic Weather Event: The Dust Bowl 1936–1940. A Web quest activity available online at: http://edweb.sdsu.edu/t2arp/quest/dustbowl/dust.html. Even if your students are too young to do this activity, it contains good resource links that will help you and your students learn about the Dust Bowl era.

Emerson, Kathi, and Susan Keeler. *This Land Is Your Land: Woody Guthrie*. Available online at: http://www.siskiyous.edu/eisenhowerarts/lessonplans/folkart.htm. A lesson plan for organizing a folk art lesson based on the book.

Schlessenger Media. *Rights and Responsibilities of United States Citizens*. United States Government Series, 2002. Appropriate for upper elementary and middle school.

The Woody Guthrie Foundation and Archives. Available online at: http://www.woodyguthrie.org. This site contains background information, photographs, lesson ideas, and more.

KIDSSOURCE: RESOURCES FOR STUDENTS

Christensen, Bonnie. *Woody Guthrie: Poet of the People*. New York: Alfred A. Knopf, 2001. ISBN 0-375-81113-3.

The Dust Bowl. Available: http://www.usd.edu/anth/epa/dust.html. This site contains pictures and a movie download.

Partridge, Elizabeth. *This Land Was Made for You and Me: The Life and Songs of Woody Guthrie*. New York: Viking, 2002. ISBN 0-670-03515-1.

This Land Is Your Land
Citizenship Worksheet

Define "Democracy" in the space below using your own words.

_____

_____

_____

_____

_____

List three ways you can act as a responsible citizen in the United States.

1. _____

   _____

2. _____

   _____

3. _____

   _____

This Land Is Your Land

What does the song This Land Is Your Land mean to you? Write your answer in the space below.

_____

_____

_____

_____

_____

_____

_____

_____

_____

_____

Courage

Life shrinks or expands in proportion to one's courage.

Anais Nin (1903–1977)
The Diary of Anais Nin
Volume 3, 1939–1944

Courage is an important and often misunderstood character trait. Sometimes courageous people are larger-than-life heroes, but often they are everyday people who stand up for what is right, even if it means doing the unpopular. Most of these people would probably not define themselves as courageous. They simply see their actions in the light of doing what had to be done. It is important for children to broaden their definition of courage beyond comic book superheroes. They need to start seeing courage in their immediate friends, in their family members, and in themselves. The books in this section are excellent for children because they feature courageous youngsters. Wodney Wat stutters in *Hooway for Wodney Wat,* a problem that has caused him considerable difficulty. In *Oliver Button Is a Sissy,* the title character doesn't enjoy the same things as the other children; he puts up with being teased and bullied while staying true to himself. Wodney Wat and Oliver Button will entertain students. These brave characters will also challenge them to broaden their definition of courage and what it means to be courageous.

Hooway for Wodney Wat by Helen Lester

To Wodney she looked especially scary. What would she do when she heard him speak? Breathe capybara breath in his face? Or tie him up in his own tail? Or even pounce on him?

Lester, Helen. *Hooway for Wodney Wat*. Illustrated by Lynn Munsinger. Boston: Houghton Mifflin Co. (Walter Lorraine Books), 1999. ISBN 0-395-92392-1.

Reading Level: 2.5

Interest Level: K–3 (Higher if tied in thematically with instruction)

The Story

Rodney Rat cannot pronounce the letter "r." When Rodney speaks, his "r's" sound like "w's." The children enjoy teasing Rodney, who pronounces his name "Wodney Wat." Embarrassed by his problem, Wodney speaks very quietly, stays to himself, and hides in his jacket. One day a new student comes to the class. Her name is Camilla Capybara. She is a bully who intimidates everyone. The story turns during a game of Simon Says, when Wodney Wat is picked to be the leader. Wodney's instructions to ". . . weed the sign," ". . . wap your paws awound your head," and, ". . . go west" cause Camilla all sorts of problems. The game ends when she hikes into the sunset never to be seen again. During the game, Wodney finds his voice and his confidence, and ultimately becomes a hero.

Character Connections

Television and movies give us the impression that courage happens in intense, dramatic moments, but this is not always the case. Children do not realize that many of the most courageous people around them are calmly facing their problems each day and coping in the best way they can. Wodney Wat gives us an excellent opportunity to focus on courage as he perseveres coming to school each day in spite of being taunted and teased. Even with his shyness and lack of confidence, he bravely comes each day to learn and grow. As you read Wodney Wat with students, use the opportunity to focus on the obvious negative behaviors in the story, but don't forget the calm, quiet courage displayed by this likable little rodent hiding in his jacket. Who knows, you might find you have some very courageous students in your room! With any luck, students will also begin to see themselves as people of courage.

About the Author

Well known for her stories that use humorous approaches to important children's issues, Helen Lester began writing when her children were young. She felt the need for more short but satisfying bedtime stories. She has gotten her ideas from her experiences as a teacher, from jokes and rhymes, and from her children as they have grown up. Her ideas usually pop into her head when she is doing unexciting things, and she tries to write them down right away. She then spends several months developing the story before turning it over to Lynn Munsinger, her illustrator. They have collaborated on more than ten books. Lester also wrote a book about writing titled *Author, A True Story*. Lester retired from teaching several years ago. She now spends her time visiting schools, cooking, running, drawing, and hiking.

About the Illustrator

Born in Greenfield, Massachusetts, in 1951, Lynn Munsinger graduated from Tufts University in 1974. She continued her studies at the Rhode Island School of Design and received a bachelor of fine arts degree in 1977. Munsinger is the illustrator of more than eighty children's books, including *Tacky the Penguin*, *What Mommies Do Best/What Daddies Do Best*, and *The Three Blind Mice Mystery*. Munsinger is a dedicated artist, whose illustrations have helped to tell the stories created by more than twenty-five authors.

Objectives

After reading this book, students will be able to

- Define related vocabulary.
- Demonstrate understanding of the story by answering related questions.
- Demonstrate understanding of courage by discussing its characteristics.
- Identify examples of courage in the life of someone they know of or know personally or from their own life experience.

Classroom Exercises

Prereading Activity

Write "What is courage?" on the chalkboard or overhead projector and ask students to brainstorm a list of things that indicate courage. Answers will probably include things such as brave, fearless, or strong, for example. Next, ask them to brainstorm a list of people they think are courageous; a variety of answers will follow and might even include some fictional characters like Superman or Spiderman, depending on your group. Ask students if they would consider someone who is very shy, stays to themselves, and hides in their jacket to be courageous. After allowing time for answers and discussion, ask students to listen to *Hooway for Wodney Wat*.

Vocabulary

Students may need help defining the following terms. Define the terms either before reading the story or, using context clues while reading, after you have finished.

shy	capybara
gnaw (gnawed)	tremble (trembling)
scurry	rodent

Comprehension and Values Questions

Select and use only those questions that are suited for your class or group. Some questions ask about story facts, but others require the students to analyze story events. Higher-level questions may bring a variety of answers; ask students to justify their response with examples from the story to support their point.

- Describe Wodney Wat.
- Why do the other rodents tease Wodney?
- How do you think Wodney feels about himself? Why does he feel this way?
- How does Wodney show his embarrassment and lack of confidence?
- Who is the new in the class? Describe her.
- How did Camilla act?
- What words can you think of to describe Camilla's behavior?
- What game did the Rodents play during the final recess? Who was picked to lead the game?
- Why was Camilla confused during the game?
- What happened to Wodney Wat during the game?
- How did Wodney feel about himself after the game? How did the other Rodents feel about him?

Character Exercises

Evaluate your class and decide if you want to do this with one or two selected students or as a whole class activity. Keep in mind the maturity and safety of your students when deciding which approach to take.

Clear a space in the room or go to an open area with level ground. Blindfold a student and ask him or her to walk from one end of the area to another. First, allow a guide to help the blindfolded student. The guide can hold the other student's arm but cannot talk or give directions. Next, allow verbal directions but no physical guidance to the blindfolded student. Finally, ask the student to walk across the space with no guidance at all.

Debrief the blindfolded student using some of the following questions:

- How did it feel not to be able to see?

- Which type of guidance did you like best, spoken directions or being guided by the arm?

- What would it have been like if you had to make it across the area without the first two guided trips?

- It is probably safe to say this experience made you a little nervous or scared, which is normal. But why would you do it? Why do we take part in things that make us feel nervous or scared?

- (Direct this to the entire class.) In life, do we ever do things that make us feel nervous or scared? Name some of these things and tell me, in your opinion, why we do them.

Point out to the class that courage is involved when we follow through with activities even when they seem a bit scary, and tie this back into the story of Wodney Wat.

Wodney exhibits courage in many ways. He goes to school even though he knows he will be teased. He does not run away when the other rodents tease him. Even though their unkindness hurts, he stands his ground and answers their questions. Note also that he does not fight with the students, even though their teasing must make him feel hurt and angry. It takes courage to control your anger. He participates in class—quietly, but he does participate. He does not run away from Camilla even though he is afraid of her. Brainstorm a list of Wodney's courageous acts with your students. They may list some of these actions or others not mentioned here.

Wodney is a very courageous rodent. His acts spring from four basic characteristics of courage. Use your list of his courageous acts and tie them into these characteristics.

- *Positive Attitude*—he has the right idea about life and what he needs to do.

- *Taking Action*—Wodney knows he needs to learn and grow so he can be a responsible grown up. He continues going to school and working in class, even though it is difficult.

- *Achievement*—Because of his attitude and actions, Wodney is learning and growing. And in the book's climax with Camilla, he saves the day.

- *Acknowledgment*—During the game of Simon Says, Wodney begins to realize he is achieving something. He instantly understands what is going on and is able to translate the events into much deserved self-congratulation. Wodney's ability to pat himself on the back is more important than the acknowledgment of his peers that comes on the book's last page. Be sure students recognize this element of the story.

Use the following characteristics of courage to discuss courage with the class. Your discussion may want to include some of the following points:

- Courage often springs from knowing that something must be done or is the right thing to do even if it is unpopular (attitude).

- Courage is not always big dramatic actions; often, in fact, courage happens in small, quiet acts that go unnoticed.

- Courage does not always lead to achievement on the first try. Often courageous people must continue to try before accomplishing their goals.

- Courageous people often do not want or seek public acknowledgment of their actions. Their personal satisfaction is all they need.

- Finally, courage is not foolishness. Rushing, without thought, into situations can make matters worse and make problems worse. Courageous people are thoughtful and careful. They do not take unnecessary chances that could endanger their lives or the lives of others.

When you are done, create a class Courage Hall of Fame using the worksheet at the end of this section. Ask each student to profile a courageous person they know, showing how that person demonstrates positive attitude, taking action, achievement, and acknowledgment. Compile the papers and display them so that students throughout the school can see them.

Integrate Your Curriculum

Art

- Ask students to draw a picture of someone displaying courage. Their picture might be a famous person, a family member, or themselves. Students may draw their picture based on the person they chose for their Courage Hall of Fame sheet and use it as an illustration accompanying the report.

Science

- Study rodents. The story specifically mentions rats, capybaras, mice, hamsters, and guinea pigs. Students will be familiar with some of these animals as pets but will not know them all. Challenge them to identify and learn about other rodent species.

Language Arts

- Possible journal topics include the following:

    - Why do you think people tease or bully other people?

    - How do you think Camilla could have avoided misunderstanding Wodney Wat?

    - Explain in your own words how Wodney Wat demonstrated courage.

Send home a separate Courage Hall of Fame sheet asking parents to fill it out, relating the four characteristics of courage to their child. Collect the returned papers and, using discretion, share them with the class in some way to help students get to know each other better, build self-esteem, and encourage mutual respect within the group.

TEACHSOURCE: RESOURCES FOR TEACHERS

Absolutely Positive.Com. *Quotes on Character, Courage and Conscience.* Available: http://pages. ivillage.com/diamond2b/quotesoncharacter.html. Interesting quotes and thought to spark class discussion.

Hamilton County School System, Chattanooga, Tennessee. *Connect to Character: Courage Websites for Teachers.* Available: http://web.utk.edu/~arox/teacherscourage.html. Provides links to multiple resources related to courage.

KIDSSOURCE: RESOURCES FOR STUDENTS

Hamilton County School System, Chattanooga, Tennessee. *Connect to Character: Courage Websites for Students.* Available: http://web.utk.edu/~arox/kidscourage.html. Provides links to multiple resources related to courage.

The Happy Capy. Available: http://www.capybara.com/capybaras/. A Web site devoted to the capybara. Students can learn about the real animal Camilla is based on.

Johnston, Marianne. *Dealing with Bullying.* The Conflict Resolution Library. New York: Rosen Publishing/PowerKids Press, 1996. ISBN 0-8239-2374-6.

Lester, Helen. *Author, A True Story.* Boston: Houghton Mifflin, 1997. ISBN 0-395-82744-2. An inspiring autobiography of the author's writing life. Children will enjoy this book.

My Hero.com. Available at: http://www.myhero.com/home.asp. An interesting Web site, it even allows students to post their own heroes.

Raatma, Lucia. *Courage.* Character Education series. Mankato, MN: Bridgestone Books, 2000. ISBN: 0-7368-0507-9.

Ricciuti, Edward R. *What on Earth Is a Capybara?* Bruce Glassman, Comp. Woodbridge, CT: Blackbirch Press, 1995. ASIN: 1567110975.

Romain, Trevor. *Bullies Are a Pain in the Brain.* Minneapolis, MN: Free Spirit, 1997. ISBN 1-57542-023-6.

Courage Hall of Fame

Select a person who you feel belongs in the Courage Hall of Fame. You may choose someone famous or someone you know. Explain how your courageous person exhibits the four characteristics of courage in the spaces below.

Paste a picture of your Courage Hall of Fame nominee here.

Name of Courage Hall of Fame member: _____

Important facts:
Give dates of the nominee's life: _____

Where did/does the nominee live? _____

What did the nominee do that qualifies him or her for the Courage Hall of Fame?

_____

Explain how your nominee demonstrated the four characteristics of courage in the spaces below.

Positive Attitude	Taking Action
Achieving	**Acknowledgment**

Oliver Button Is a Sissy by Tomie dePaola

But the boys, especially the older ones, in the schoolyard teased Oliver Button. "What are those shiny shoes, sissy?" they asked.

dePaola, Tomie. *Oliver Button Is a Sissy*. New York: Harcourt Brace Jovanovich, 1979. ISBN 0-15-257852-8.

Reading Level: 2.8

Interest Level: K–3 (Higher if tied in thematically with instruction)

The Story

Oliver Button is not interested in the same things as other boys. Organized sports like baseball or football do not appeal to him. Oliver likes to draw, read, and, most of all, Oliver Button likes to dance. The boys at school tease him and call him a sissy. The girls stick up for him. His parents aren't sure what to think but decide to send him to Ms. Leah's Dancing School. Oliver excels at tap dancing, and soon Ms. Leah encourages him to enroll in a talent show competition. At school, on the Friday before the talent contest, Oliver's teacher tells the whole class about the show. Once again, his classmates tease Oliver Button. When he does not win the contest, Oliver feels embarrassed to return to school. Yet when he arrives at the schoolyard, Oliver Button discovers he has won something even more important than the talent competition.

Character Connections

Oliver exhibits many special talents that make him unique. The other children tease him because of these differences, but Oliver courageously follows his own path. This courage makes him noteworthy. He is not blind to the taunting of his classmates. The story makes it obvious that his feelings are hurt. It would be easy to imagine Oliver Button giving up his dancing lessons and trying to fit in with the other boys, but he does not. This is a great story for teaching children about the value of courage, especially if readers apply its message to themselves. Shakespeare wrote, "To thine own self be true." Oliver Button is true to himself and ultimately earns the respect of his peers because of his tenacious self-respect.

About the Author and Illustrator

Author and illustrator Tomie dePaola was born in 1934 and grew up during the end of the Great Depression. He was interested in art from a young age and says he wanted to be an artist from the time he was four years old. His family encouraged this dream. One memorable Christmas, when he was nine years old, his parents gave him nothing but art supplies.

After high school, dePaola attended Pratt Institute graduating with a bachelor of fine arts degree in 1956. Since graduating, dePaola has gone on to earn his master's degree and a doctoral equivalency. Besides writing and illustrating books for children, dePaola also does theatre work and has taught art. This talented artist has received numerous awards for his books and continues to delight audiences around the world with his wonderful children's books.

Objectives

After reading this book, students will be able to

- Demonstrate understanding of the story by answering related questions.
- Identify positive and negative character traits exhibited by characters in the story.
- Explain how Oliver Button exhibits courage and self-respect.
- Identify a courageous event from their life.
- Discuss negative aspects of name-calling and bullying behaviors.

Classroom Exercises

Prereading Activity

Make a two-column chart on your board or overhead. Label one side "boys" and the other side "girls." Ask students to list things that boys do and things that girls do. List the suggestions in the appropriate column. Despite efforts in recent years to end gender stereotyping, your lists will probably reflect traditional roles for boys and girls. When you reach an ending point, ask the students what they would call a boy who liked to jump rope, play with paper dolls, dress up, and, most of all—dance. List the responses on the board in a separate column. Read the story. Save the list of names for use after reading the story and for one of the language arts activities listed in this section.

Vocabulary

Students may need help defining the following terms. Define the words before reading or, using context clues while reading, when you are done.

tap shoes	routine
tap dance	accordion
practice	master of ceremonies

Comprehension and Values Questions

Select and use only those questions that are suited for your class or group. Some questions ask about story facts, but others require the students to analyze story events. Higher-level questions may bring a variety of answers; ask students to justify their response with examples from the story to support their point.

- How is Oliver Button different from the other boys? Give examples of things he does that show he is different.
- How do the other children react to Oliver Button? Do you think they are right to react the way they do?
- Why do Mama and Papa enroll Oliver in Ms. Leah's Dancing School?
- How do the boys at school react to Oliver's dancing lessons?
- What does Ms. Leah suggest Oliver enter?
- Who wins the talent show contest?
- How does Oliver feel about losing? Give some examples from the story to explain your answer.
- When Oliver arrives at school, what does he find on the school wall?
- What do you think the new writing on the wall means?

Character Exercises

Before doing the exercise that follows, refer back to the list of names. Ask students if Oliver Button really is any of the things on the third list. Hold a brief discussion about name-calling and bullying, pointing out that it is bad for both the bully and victim. Change the direction of the discussion back to Oliver Button. Ask students how they think Oliver felt when students made fun of him. Ask them why they think Oliver Button didn't try to change but continued doing the things he enjoyed. Help the students understand that Oliver Button had courage. His courage helped him persevere, continuing to practice his tap dancing and doing the things he enjoyed. Ask the students if they think they have courage like Oliver Button. Encourage those who are willing to share individual acts of courage to do so. To wrap up the discussion, assure students that even if they do not realize it, they have courage and are brave. To help reinforce this concept, do the Courage Tight-Rope Walk exercise:

Get several long pieces of blue butcher paper to represent water and lay them out on the floor of your classroom. Attach a long piece of rope or colored tape down the middle of the paper. Make some signs that say "Your Life" and tape them to each end of the rope.

Give each child three pieces of paper, each of a different color. One of the colors represents problems or bad things that can happen to people. The second piece represents good things, people, or experiences that are a part of our lives. The third piece is to be something unique to that child, a personal trait. It might be a special talent, hobby, friendship, strength or some other unique personal treasure. Students should write or draw on the appropriate colored paper their response choice to each category. For example, Oliver Button might draw a picture of the school bullies on his problem paper. On the good things paper, he might draw a picture of his parents, and, on the personal trait paper, he might draw a picture of himself tap-dancing.

When students are done with their drawings, allow a brief time for sharing. There will probably be several similar things in the problem and good things categories. Hopefully, this will help students realize that they are not alone in facing difficulties. Direct students to lay their papers on the floor. Place all the problems on one side of the line and the good things papers on the other. Divide the students into two groups, with each group stationed at opposite ends of the tightrope.

Explain to students that we all have good and bad experiences in our lives. Assure them that we can get through these experiences. The good things and people in our lives can help us, but we can also help ourselves by relying on our unique strengths, gifts, and talents. Each student then walks the tightrope, carrying his or her personal trait paper to symbolize the unique talents that helps them get through life. Before the first child walks the tightrope, hand him or her one more card to carry across the rope. On this card, write the word *courage* in big letters. Explain to the student that he or she has courage like Oliver Button, and this courage will also help the student get through life.

Alternate group members walking back and forth across the life tightrope until each student has walked across. As students cross the tightrope, they hand the "courage" card off to the next person, telling that person that he or she also has courage and that it will help him or her get through life. Continue until all students have walked the tightrope of life carrying their personal talents and courage with them.

When you are done, remind students that they all have courage and that they use it every day. Encourage them to think of themselves as strong, brave, and courageous people.

Integrate Your Curriculum

Performing Arts

- Study tap dance. Locate a local dance school or theatre to arrange for a visiting artist who will demonstrate this dance style for students and teach them a few basic moves. Locate a few old movies such as *That's Entertainment* that feature tap dancing to show the students. (Note: preview the videos and select only what is appropriate for this lesson and your students.)

- Put on a class talent show. Allow those students who want to participate to demonstrate a unique individual talent. Students who choose not to participate in the talent show can perform other duties, such as creating programs, writing invitations to parents and school staff, or acting as ushers. Recognize everyone with a certificate of participation for collaborating on the project.

Language Arts

- Change-to-Praise Exercise: Using your list of insulting names from the prereading activity or additional names the students supply, assign each student a name and challenge them to create a complimentary acrostic poem using the letters of the insulting word. For example "sissy" might be turned into the following acrostic:

Super

Intelligent

Superior

Savvy

You!

Post the acrostics where others can see them to challenge student conceptions about these negative words and name-calling.

PARENTZONE:
TAKING THE LESSON HOME

Send home with students the Oliver Button Courage Worksheet at the end of this section. Ask parents to discuss and debate the five courage questions with their child and help them rate the amount of courage each will take. Students can write the response paragraph themselves and return it for homework credit.

TEACHSOURCE:
RESOURCES FOR TEACHERS

Hechtel, Bob. *Tomie dePaola*. Available: http://www.bingley.com/. An unofficial Web site maintained by Hechtel, who works with Tomie dePaola.

KIDSSOURCE:
RESOURCES FOR STUDENTS

Adams, Lisa K. *Dealing with Teasing*. The Conflict Resolution Library. New York: Rosen Publishing/ PowerKids Press, 1997. ISBN 0-8239-5070-0.

Educational Paperback Association. *Tomie dePaola*. Available: http://www.edupaperback.org/ authorbios/Depaola_Tomie.html. Contains biography information about the author.

Ellman, Barbara, and Tomie dePaola. *Tomie dePaola: His Art and His Stories*. New York: G. P. Putnam's Sons, 1999. ISBN 0-399-23129-3.

Grunsell, Angela. *Bullying*. Let's Talk About series. New York: Gloucester Press, 1989. ISBN 0-531-17213-9.

I Want to Be a Dancer. I Want to Be series. New York: Harcourt Brace, 1997. ISBN 0-15-201299-0. A general book about many different types of dance.

Johnson, Julie. *How do I Feel about Bullies and Gangs*. Brookfield, CT: Copper Beech Books, 1998. ISBN 0-7613-0807-5.

Jones, Bill T., and Susan Kuklin. *Dance*. Photographed by Susan Kuklin. New York: Hyperion Books for Children, 1998. ISBN 0-7868-2307-0. This book provides insight into basic concepts of dance through poetic text and beautiful photographs.

Oliver Button has courage!

Directions: After reading and talking about Oliver Button Is a Sissy, list three ways that Oliver Button showed courage in the spaces below:

1. _____

_____

2. _____

_____

3. _____

_____

I have courage too!

Now list three times that you showed courage in the spaces below. Be prepared to share your experiences with the class.

1. _____

_____

2. _____

_____

3. _____

_____

Oliver Button Characters

The characters in Oliver Button's story have positive and negative character traits. Think about these characters and fill in examples from the story that show good and bad things about each character.
<u>HINT:</u> Some characters will have both positive and negative traits, some might have only one side filled in. Think about the story and characters as you answer!

Negative Actions	Character	Positive Actions
Sample:		
Almost let his hurt get the best of him by not wanting to go to school after he lost the contest.	Oliver Button	Displayed courage by being himself even when people teased and bullied him.
	Boys at school	
	Papa	
	Girls at school	

Oliver Button Courage Worksheet

Directions: You can do this worksheet in class or take it home and use it as a discussion starter with your parents.

Read, think, and respond to the following statements. Show your thoughts by circling the number on the opinion scale on the right.

How much courage does it take to	Very Hard		Somewhat Hard		Not Hard at all
1. confront a bully who is your age and is teasing a younger kid?	1	2	3	4	5
2. tell your teacher about someone who is bullying you or another student?	1	2	3	4	5
3. do something you know is right or fun even if people make fun of you?	1	2	3	4	5
4. start over again after you have made a mistake or failed at something?	1	2	3	4	5
5. tell the truth even when you know you might get in trouble?	1	2	3	4	5

Which of the above would be the hardest for you? Which would be the easiest? Which is the most important? Pick one of these questions and explain it in a paragraph written in the space below. Use the back of this paper if you need more space.

_____

_____

_____

_____

_____

3

Friendship

Friendship makes prosperity more shining and lessens adversity by dividing and sharing it.

Cicero (106–43 B.C.)
On Friendship, 44 B.C.

The virtue of friendship is worth looking at in any character education program. What does it mean to be friends? How do we become friends? Children often do not understand that friendship is an ongoing, evolving relationship that forms over time. *Enemy Pie* provides an excellent look into how we meet and become friends from a child's perspective. Use it at the start of the school year when students don't know each other or when a new student is added to the group during the year. It will provoke discussion and understanding about the true nature of friendship.

Enemy Pie by Derek Munson

It was at this point that I panicked. I didn't want Jeremy to eat Enemy Pie! He was my friend! I couldn't let him eat it.

Munson, Derek. *Enemy Pie*. Illustrated by Tara Calahan King. San Francisco: Chronicle Books, 2000. ISBN 0-8118-2778-X.

Reading Level: 2.7

Interest Level: K–3 (Higher if tied in thematically with instruction)

The Story

A boy's perfect summer is ruined when someone moves into the neighborhood. The new boy laughs at him and seems to be stealing his best friend. For the first time in his life, he has an enemy. His understanding father agrees to help by making an enemy pie. When the pie is done, his father tells him that to make the pie work, he must first lure his enemy over and spend the day with him. The boy decides that he can spend one day with his enemy knowing that afterward the new boy will be out of his life forever. As the boys spend the day together, they discover they have much in common and enjoy each other's company. When the time comes to eat the enemy pie, the protagonist must make a quick decision: does he really want his new neighbor—and friend—to eat it?

Character Connections

Enemy Pie is a book about cooperation and communication, and ultimately about friendship. The story also possesses a good lesson in conflict management because of the father's wise approach to dealing with the perceived enemy. By involving his son in making an enemy pie, the father creates a situation that forces the boy to reach out to his enemy. In doing so, he finds a friend. We often forget that true friendships form over time as we share life's events with each other. Children are often perplexed when it comes to understanding and valuing other people while seeking new friends. *Enemy Pie* helps all readers understand and reflect on the value we should place on getting to know one another as we grow in friendship together.

About the Author

Fascinated with the artistic process and inspired by all things unusual, Derek Munson began his writing habit at age twenty with a focus on philosophy and imagination. His playful nature, respect for children, and a daydream while picking blackberries resulted in the creation of *Enemy Pie*, his first published book. Currently his work is based on the study and teaching of the creative experience. When he is not writing, Munson enjoys novice status in the study of aikido, chess, skateboarding, and physics. He was born and raised in Redmond, Washington, and lives there today with his wife, Suzanne, and their daughter, Abigail.

About the Illustrator

Tara Calahan King is currently illustrating her forth children's book, *Four Boys Named Jordan* (Penguin Books), written by the actress and children's songwriter Jessica Harper (expected publication is July 2004). In addition to *Enemy Pie*, King's illustrations are featured in other award-winning titles, including *Odd Velvet* (Chronicle Books) by Mary E. Whitcomb and *Superhero Max* (Random House) by Lawrence David. She enjoys visiting and reading her books to children at local schools in her area. This is where she finds inspiration for her characters. Her work is known and loved for its saturated colors, odd perspectives, and quirky, big-headed characters. She renders the illustrations in her books using colored pencil and chalk pastels, with the addition of collage in her upcoming book. She also illustrates for teen and adult publications and paints murals of all kinds. King lives in Cincinnati, Ohio, with her husband Rick and her two children, Ricky and Emma. She is a stay-at-home mom who has incorporated her passion for illustrating into her lifestyle, which has become a dream come true.

Objectives

After reading this book, students will be able to

• Define related vocabulary.

• Demonstrate understanding of the story by answering related questions.

• Explain in their own words what friendship means to them.

• Explain how they might try to make a new friend.

Classroom Activities

Prereading Activity

After showing students the cover of the book ask them the following questions to lead into the story:

• What is an enemy?

• If you were making an enemy pie, what types of ingredients would you put in it?

• What do you think will happen in this story?

Vocabulary

Students may need help defining the following terms. Define the terms either before reading the story or, using context clues while reading, after you have finished.

enemy	boomerang
perfect	ingredients
trampoline	confused

Comprehension and Values Questions

Select and use only those questions that are suited to your class or group. Some questions ask about story facts, but others require the students to analyze story events. Higher-level questions may bring a variety of answers; ask students to justify their response with examples from the story to support their point.

- Name three reasons it should have been a perfect summer for the boy in the story.
- What happened that ruined the perfect summer?
- What did Jeremy Ross do that made the storyteller feel he was his enemy?
- Where did our storyteller post the enemy list?
- How is the boy's father going to help him get rid of the enemy?
- What did the boy expect enemy pie to be like?
- When it was done, was the enemy pie like he expected it would be? How was it different and why did Dad say the pie had to seem good?
- What did the boy have to do to make the enemy pie work?
- List three things the boy and Jeremy did together.
- Do you think it was easy spending the day with Jeremy? How do you think the boy felt?
- As the boys spent the day together the storyteller's feelings changed. How and why did his feelings change?
- What did Dad serve the boys for dinner?
- What happened when Dad served the enemy pie?
- What did the boys plan to do the next day?
- Do you think the boys will become real friends? Why or why not?

Character Exercises

Exercise 1: Blindfold Exercise. You will need a blindfold and two volunteers (preferably from outside the class, perhaps two older students or adult members of the school staff who are willing to play along). Bring in the first volunteer and blindfold him or her. Now bring in the second volunteer and introduce this person to the blindfolded helper as his or her new best friend. The blindfolded person should immediately respond that he or she disagrees and in fact doesn't like the person. The blindfolded volunteer may even offer a reason or two and insist on not liking the other person even when the teacher points out that he or she is blindfolded and doesn't even know who the other person is. Enlist student thoughts and reactions about the blindfolded person's quick judgment. You may want to use these questions to guide a class discussion or make up some of your own:

- Do you think (*name of blindfolded volunteer*) was right to judge (*name of second volunteer*) when she (he) didn't even know who it was?
- How could (blindfolded volunteer) have found out more about (second volunteer)?

- When you meet someone for the first time, even though you can see the person, how is it like what (blindfolded volunteer) experienced?

Note: the purpose of this exercise is to point out to students that even when we can see someone, we do not really know the person. The boy in Enemy Pie had been around Jeremy, but he still did not know him. Knowing someone takes time, patience, and effort. Follow this role-play example with the Getting to Know You worksheets accompanying this section.

Exercise 2: Getting to Know You. Pair each student with someone in the class that he or she does not know well. Direct students to fill in the Getting to Know You worksheet by interviewing each other. After the interviews, students should reflect on what they learned about their classmates by filling in the graphic organizer worksheet included in this section and writing a brief paragraph in response to the writing prompt. Develop and assign partner activities periodically, using the same pairings to help students get to know each other over a longer period of time. These activities could be assignments or nonacademic activities such as doing service projects together or being line buddies or key pals.

Exercise 3: Friendship Pie. As a concluding activity, ask students to fill in the Friendship Pie worksheet by listing ingredients that make a good friendship. Answers will vary but should include things such as "friends listen to each other," "friends respect each other," "friends share with each other," and so on.

Integrate Your Curriculum

Art

- Using a piece of butcher paper, draw and color a large enemy pie in the center. Then allow the students to draw imaginary enemy pie ingredients on their own paper. Cut the ingredients out and glue them around the pie in a collage. Label each persons ingredients. Post the *Enemy Pie* collage somewhere in the room or on a bulletin board.

Science and Math

- Make a pie with your class. Allow students to measure ingredients, reviewing math skills in the process. Discuss the ingredients and how they react to temperature when cooked to form the pie. Discuss the nutritional value of the pie, perhaps comparing the nutritional values of several types of pies. Eat the pie when done.

Language Arts

- Have students write in their journals on topics such as the following:
  - Write about a friend that you did not like when you first met each other. What was it about the person that you disliked and how did he or she become your friend?
  - Tell about a time that one of your parents or someone else helped you realize that you were wrong about another person or thing.
  - Think about Jeremy Ross. How do you think he felt as the new kid in the neighborhood? Do you think he considered the narrator his enemy?
  - What have you learned about making friends and about friendship by reading *Enemy Pie* and doing the Getting to Know You interview and exercise?

Social Studies

- The boys play with a boomerang. Study the history of this toy, focusing on its Australian origins. How was the boomerang first used? How are boomerangs used today? If possible, find someone who understands boomerangs and invite this person to demonstrate correct throwing techniques for the class.

ParentZone: Taking the Lesson Home

Ask parents to have a family storytelling time in which family members recount how they met their best friend. They could then discuss the importance of not relying on first impressions when judging someone or something. Conclude the discussion with each family member filling in the blanks in the following statements: I was really wrong about _____ when I first got to know her (him). I thought she (he) was _____, but when I learned more about her (him), I learned she (he) was really _____.

TeachSource: Resources for Teachers

Stanton, Jane. Tara Calahan King: Book Illustrator. *Art Academy News.* Available: http://www.artacademy.edu/kingLW01.htm. This profile of Tara Calahan King profiles the illustrator's visit to the Art Academy of Cincinnati.

KidsSource: Resources for Students

Derek Munson Author Chat. Available: http://www.authorchats.com. Students may enjoy reading this archived chat between Derek Munson and an elementary and a middle school class.

<u>Getting to Know You</u>
Don't make an enemy pie,
make a new friend instead!

Directions: Ask your partner the questions below
and write their answers in the spaces provided.

1. What is your full name?

    _____

2. Do you have any pets? If so, what kind(s) and what are their names?

    _____

3. What games do you like to play? (Any type of game or sport.)

    _____

4. What kinds of music do you like to listen to? _____

5. What is your favorite thing about school? _____

6. What do you do in your free time? _____

7. What is your favorite TV show? _____

8. What is your favorite movie? _____

9. What is your favorite food? _____

10. What do you want to be when you grow up? _____

Read over the answers you wrote down. How would you answer the same
questions? Do you and your partner have anything in common? What? How are
you alike? How are you different? Talk about these things with your partner
and be ready to share your thoughts with your teacher and class.

<u>Getting to Know You</u>

How are we alike? How are we different?

Directions: Use your interview sheet to fill in the graphic organizer below showing how you and your partner are alike and different.

My Partner: _____

Me: _____

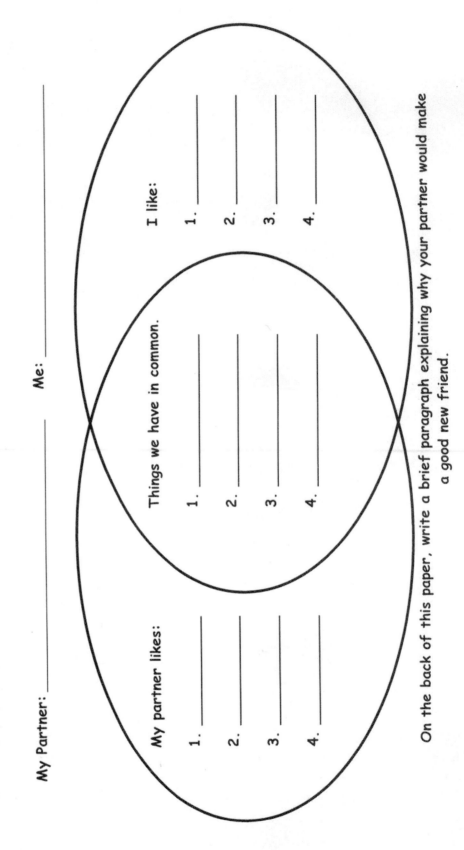

I like:

1. _____
2. _____
3. _____
4. _____

Things we have in common.

1. _____
2. _____
3. _____
4. _____

My partner likes:

1. _____
2. _____
3. _____
4. _____

On the back of this paper, write a brief paragraph explaining why your partner would make a good new friend.

Making a Friendship Pie!

Directions: List ingredients for a good friendship pie in the space below.

My Friendship Pie!

Ingredients: (Example) Listening—Good friends <u>listen</u> to each other.

1. _____

2. _____

3. _____

4. _____

5. _____

4

Honesty

No legacy is so rich as honesty.

William Shakespeare (1564–1616)
All's Well That Ends Well
Act 3, Scene 5

Honesty is the best policy. Hopefully, we all believe this, but we live in a world filled with shades of gray. *What's So Terrible about Swallowing an Apple Seed?* points to the complexities of living an honest life when two sisters become involved in a seemingly innocent cycle of lies. The story points to a fundamental truth about being honest in a lighthearted and entertaining way. It will provide your students with good discussion opportunities and the chance to consider and define their own understanding of this important value.

What's So Terrible about Swallowing an Apple Seed?

by Harriet Lerner and Susan Goldhor

Katie thought fast. "Well," she said, trying to sound smart, "that apple seed is going to grow into a tree right inside your stomach. That's what's so terrible."

Lerner, Harriet, and Susan Goldhor. *What's So Terrible about Swallowing an Apple Seed?* Illustrated by Catherine O'Neill. New York: HarperCollins, 1996. ISBN 0-06-024524-7.

Reading Level: 2.8

Interest Level: K–3 (Higher if tied in thematically with instruction)

The Story

Rosie and her big sister Katie are enjoying a day in their favorite apple tree. When Rosie accidentally swallows a seed, Katie tells her an apple tree will grow in her stomach. Doubtful at first, Rosie believes Katie and begins to imagine her life with tree branches growing out her ears. Instead of confessing the truth, Katie adds to Rosie's fantasy by claiming to see the tips of branches in her ears and pointing out advantages of the imaginary tree limbs. Accepting her situation, Rosie confides her news to a friend, who immediately tells her she sees nothing in her ears but " a little ear dirt." Both girls come to terms with the truth, and the story ends happily as Katie tells Rosie a bedtime story.

Character Connections

This story about the importance of honesty uses a light whimsical tone to get its point across. Katie's lie is not told maliciously but serves to point out the dangers of not presenting the truth in all situations. Rosie experiences real anxiety while waiting for her branches to sprout, and Katie, not knowing how to get out of the situation, helps the lie to grow. When confronted by the truth, Rosie reacts angrily and is disappointed in the big sister she trusted. Katie is defensive but relieved. Both girls are able to resolve their feelings, but each has gained new insight into the importance of honesty in their relationship.

About the Authors

Harriet Lerner (left) and Susan Goldhor (right) are sisters who were born in Brooklyn, New York. When the girls were growing up, learning and culture played an important role in their family. Their parents were Russian-Jewish immigrants who instilled in them a love of art and creativity. They were frequent visitors to the Brooklyn Public Library and Brooklyn Botanical Garden. These marvelous places helped to reinforce the values that Susan and Harriet learned at home.

As the sisters grew, they picked different career paths. Goldhor, the oldest, is a biologist and researcher in Cambridge, Massachusetts. Her research projects include recycling organic wastes into a variety of products and exploring what fish like to eat. Lerner, who lives in Lawrence, Kansas, is a well-known psychologist specializing in the psychology of women and family relationships. In addition to writing children's books, Lerner is well known as the author of books for adults, including the *New York Times* bestseller, *The Dance of Anger.*

What's So Terrible about Swallowing an Apple Seed? was Lerner and Goldhor's first collaboration. Since its publication, they have co-authored two additional children's books.

About the Illustrator

Catherine O'Neill lives in Ithaca, New York. She studied art at the University of Michigan. Catherine received her master's degree from Cornell University. She is the illustrator of ten children's books, including *The Luck of the Irish* and her own title *Mrs. Dunphy's Dog.* Also a talented cartoonist, O'Neill's cartoons are frequently featured in magazines and newspapers.

Objectives

After reading this book, students will be able to

• Demonstrate understanding of the story by answering related questions.

• Identify the feelings of each character in the story.

• List reasons why honesty is important.

Classroom Exercises

Prereading Activity

Locate a pack of edible seeds; invite students who are willing to eat one. After students have eaten the seeds, ask them what they think will happen to the seeds? Do they think the seeds could sprout and grow inside their stomachs? After a brief, hopefully fun, discussion, begin reading the story.

Comprehension and Values Questions

Select and use only those questions that are suited to your class or group. Some questions ask about story facts, but others require the students to analyze story events. Higher-level questions may bring a variety of answers; ask students to justify their response with examples from the story to support their point.

- What did Rosie do when she and Katie were eating apples in the tree?
- What did Katie tell Rosie about swallowing the seeds?
- Was Rosie happy about the apple tree growing inside her?
- What problems did Rosie imagine about the tree?
- Why was it hard for Katie to tell Rosie the truth?
- What are some of the things Katie told Rosie to cheer her up?
- How did Rosie discover the truth about her apple tree?
- How did Rosie feel when she knew the truth?
- How did Katie feel when Rosie confronted her with the truth?
- Why do you think Rosie missed her apple tree at the end of the story?

Character Exercises

To do this exercise, you will need two large balls of string or yarn and two copies of the Character Exercise Script included at the end of this chapter. Ask for two volunteers from the class. The volunteers will role-play Rosie and Katie from the story by reading the Character Exercise Script. The other students will sit in a circle around the volunteers. Select two class members sitting in the circle and give both students one of the balls of string. Instruct the students in the outer circle to toss the balls of string gently across the circle to a different student each time the Katie character tells a lie during the scene. The students tossing the string should also hold onto the string before they toss the ball so that a web of string builds up around the two actors in the middle of the circle.

This exercise visually illustrates what happens to people who don't tell the truth; they become caught in a web of lies. Be sure to point out to the students that Rosie is also caught in the web, even though she did not lie. It is important for students to understand that our lies also affect others.

Integrate Your Curriculum

Art

- Ask the children to imagine some of the problems or benefits they might encounter if they had an apple tree growing out their ears. Direct them to illustrate one of their ideas showing what might happen.

Science

- If apples grow in your area, arrange to visit an orchard to learn how they grow. If not, study where apples grow and what conditions are ideal for fruit production. Bring in a variety of apples such as Red Delicious, Rome, Granny Smith, and Fuji. Have the students identify the differences between the various types, including shape, color, size, taste, acidity, and so on. Compare the findings and predict how the fruit characteristics might affect their use. Study products made with apples and see if any of the varieties are better suited to one use or another.

Language Arts

- Using the artwork created in art class, have students write a short paragraph explaining their tree picture. What problem or benefit does it show? Why do they think this would be a problem or benefit? Can they imagine a way to solve the situation if it is a problem? If the picture portrays a benefit, do they feel it outweighs the inconvenience of having an apple tree growing out of their ears?

- Possible journal prompts:
    - Explain why honesty is always the best policy.
    - Write about a time when you were caught in a lie. What happened? Did it end as nicely as the apple seed story?
- Locate several folktales or fables that share a theme or moral based on honesty. After reading and discussing the stories with the students, divide them into small groups. Assign each group to create an original story about the importance of honesty. Student groups can write and illustrate their stories and then share them with the class.

Math

- Divide the students into groups. Give each group a dozen apples. Use the apples to review simple addition, subtraction, division, and fractions by having students group the apples to discover problem answers.

Send home a copy of the *Family Honesty Inventory* worksheet. Ask parents to do it with their children and discuss the importance of honesty within the family.

Apple Farming for Kids. Video, 30 min. Rainbow Communications, 1997. ISBN 1-887102-72-8.

KidsSource:
Resources For Students

Adams, Lisa K. *Dealing with Lying*. The Conflict Resolution Library. New York: Rosen Publishing/PowerKids Press, 1997. ISBN 0-8239-5071-9.

Gibbons, Gail. *Apples*. New York: Holiday House, 2000. ISBN 0-8234-1497-3.

Micucci, Charles. *The Life and Times of the Apple*. New York: Orchard Books, 1992. ISBN 0-531-08539-2.

Patent, Dorothy Hinshaw. *Apple Trees*. Photographs by William Muñoz. Minneapolis, MN: Lerner, 1997. ISBN 0-8225-3020-1.

Raatma, Lucia. *Honesty*. Character Education Series. Mankato, MN: Bridgestone Books, 2000. ISBN 07368-0369-6.

Character Exercise Script

Rosie: Oops, I swallowed an apple seed!
Katie: Oh, no! It's going to grow in your stomach.

(Pause to toss string balls)

Rosie: No that won't happen . . . will it?
Katie: Sure it will, your stomach is a great place for things to grow.

(Pause to toss string balls)

Rosie: Well if you say so . . .
Katie: I do—when the tree gets big enough, branches will come out of your ears.

(Pause to toss string balls)

Rosie: Hey, I think I feel something. Look in my ears; can you see anything?
Katie: I think I see branches—your tree is starting to grow!

(Pause to toss string balls)

Rosie: I don't want an apple tree growing out of my ears.
Katie: Oh, it will be fun! You can get fresh apples anytime you want them.

(Pause to toss string balls)

Rosie: Well, I do like apples.
Katie: And we will always have shade when we go to the beach.

(Pause to toss string balls)

Rosie: That's true . . . I guess.
Katie: And all our friends will be able to play on your branches.

(Pause to toss string balls)

Rosie: OK . . . maybe it will be all right.
Katie: It will be fun Rosie, just wait and see. (Toss string balls – final time)

What's So Terrible about Swallowing an Apple Seed?
Feelings Chart

Directions: After reading the story, think about what happened to Rosie and Katie because of the lie Katie told. Think about how the girls must have felt and give your responses in the spaces below.

Story Event	Character Response	
	Rosie	Katie
Katie tells Rosie the apple tree will grow in her stomach.	Sample: Doubtful but a little worried.	Sample: Bothered by what she did, but not enough to admit it.
Each night Katie tells Rosie she can see the tree branches in her ears.		
Katie does not know how to tell Rosie the truth, so she makes up more lies.		
Rosie finds out the truth—there is no apple tree!		
Katie tells Rosie she is sorry about lying to her.		

There is an old saying that states, "Honesty is the best policy." On the back of this paper explain why the saying is true.

What's So Terrible about Swallowing an Apple Seed?
<u>Family Honesty Inventory</u>

Talk about and respond to the situations below. Think about your level of honesty. Circle your response to each question. Talk about why honesty is important in your family and in life.

You admit it when you are wrong or make a mistake.

Always   Sometimes   Needs Improvement

You do not use "half-truths."

Always   Sometimes   Needs Improvement

You do not withhold information from each other.

Always   Sometimes   Needs Improvement

You do not exaggerate or minimize details.

Always   Sometimes   Needs Improvement

You discuss problems honestly to seek solutions that are fair to everyone.

Always   Sometimes   Needs Improvement

You do not manipulate information to get your own way.

Always   Sometimes   Needs Improvement

5

Perseverance and Patience

*Few things are impossible to diligence and skill.
Great works are performed not by strength, but perseverance.*

Samuel Johnson (1709–1784)

The very act of being in school requires students' perseverance. Yet they often do not understand this, and many are willing to give up on difficult tasks all too quickly. The two books in this section present different faces of perseverance and patience. *America's Champion Swimmer* presents a heroine who achieved a great athletic feat, overcoming societal odds and defeat on her first attempt. *Rocks in His Head* is the story of a father quietly persevering through difficult times to provide for his family and remain true to himself and his interests. Together these books provide a background for discussion about types of perseverance and patience. They help to show how perseverance and patience work together, and they help students understand the important role these character traits play in their lives.

America's Champion Swimmer: Gertrude Ederle

by David A. Adler

Trudy continued to fight the tide and the constant stinging spray of water in her face. She knew she would either swim the Channel or drown.

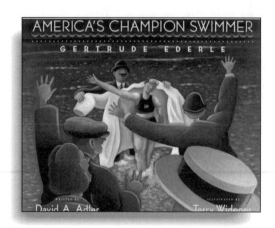

Adler, David A. *America's Champion Swimmer: Gertrude Ederle*. Illustrated by Terry Widener. New York: Gulliver Books, 2000. ISBN 0-15-201969-3.

Reading Level: 4.0

Interest Level: K–3 (Higher if tied in thematically with instruction)

The Story

Gertrude Ederle loved to swim. Born in 1906, she lived during a time when women were considered the weaker sex and not encouraged to participate in athletics. Trudy, as her friends called her, would not be stopped, however. She was determined to be the best swimmer and at the age of seventeen won three medals in the 1924 Summer Olympic Games. She earned twenty-nine U.S. and world records by the time she was nineteen. Trudy set a goal of becoming the first woman to swim the English Channel. The twenty-one-mile swim crossed cold, choppy water between England and France. Many men had attempted this treacherous swim, and only a few succeeded. People said it would be too much for her, but Trudy proved them wrong. Her fourteen-hour, thirty-one-minute swim beat the men's record by almost two hours and proved that women were capable of great athletic accomplishments.

Character Connections

Trudy's first attempt to swim the channel ended in failure. The defeat must have been difficult to handle. It confirmed what the world had been saying: a woman could not make the difficult cross-Channel swim. Trudy, however, did not give up. Instead, she found another trainer and set to work. Almost a year after her first attempt, she set foot again in the icy waters on the coast of France and began to swim for England. During the second swim, a terrible storm blew in. At times she could not see the guide boats that accompanied her. When her leg stiffened and she had trouble kicking, her trainer tried to get her to quit. She refused. Trudy had no intention of stopping, and her continued efforts resulted in triumph. Trudy's actions modeled determination and perseverance. Her story is a reminder to everyone that continued effort and vision are required to accomplish things, big and small, in our lives.

About the Author

David Adler did not start out to be a writer. He majored in economics in college and taught math in an intermediate school after he graduated. During this time, he also went to graduate school, earning a master's in business administration and then working on his doctorate. It was at this point that the inspiration for his first book *A Little at a Time* came from his nephew, who continually asked him questions. This is where the dreamer in Adler came out. He sent his manuscript out to publishers, and Random House accepted it. He continued teaching math, but he began to work on writing as a second career. Five years after his first book was published, he left teaching to write full time. Adler feels that he has been fortunate because writing allows him to pursue his many interests. He has written books on math, science, history, Jewish holidays, and more. His work also includes picture books, biographies, mysteries, and adventure stories. Adler is the author of more than seventy books for children and has received many awards for his writing.

About the Illustrator

Terry Widener lives with his wife, their three children, and an assortment of dogs and cats in McKinney, Texas. He was born in Tulsa, Oklahoma. He became a graphic designer after graduating with a degree in fine arts from the University of Tulsa but always included illustration in his work. He illustrated his first children's book in 1997 and has worked on several projects for various publishers since that time. Widener feels that children's books today feature many artistic styles, making them more exciting for the reader. He hopes his illustrations create a beautiful book and help to make the author's words come alive visually.

Objectives

After reading this book, students will be able to

- Define related vocabulary.
- Demonstrate understanding of the story by answering related questions.
- Identify a goal they would like to achieve and list steps they will have to do to accomplish the goal.
- Explain in their own words why it is important to persevere in difficult situations.
- Write an acrostic poem about the importance of perseverance.

Classroom Exercises

Prereading Activity

Give balloons to the students and ask them to blow them up. This will be easier for some students and more difficult for others. Encourage the students who are having trouble by showing them strategies such as pulling and stretching the balloon by hand to help loosen up the balloon. Have them try again until they accomplish the goal of blowing up their balloons.

Hold a brief class discussion built around the following questions:

- For those that had trouble blowing up their balloons, how did it feel when you were not successful? Did anyone give up trying? Why? For those who kept trying to blow up their balloon, why didn't you give up? How did it feel when you finally blew up the balloon?

- For those who blew up their balloons with no trouble, why do you think you were able to blow up your balloon so quickly? How did it make you feel to be able to do the task so easily? Can you think of something you wanted to do that was not as easy as blowing up the balloon? What was it and were you able to do it?

After the class discussion show the students the book and tell them you are going to share a story about a woman who wanted to accomplish a very difficult goal.

Vocabulary

Students may need help defining the following terms. Define the terms either before reading the story or, using context clues while reading, after you have finished.

disaster	poised	lanolin
dog paddle	Olympic Games	reporter
courageous	English Channel	photographer
determined	bathing cap	flare
modest	goggles	foghorn

Comprehension and Values Questions

Select and use only those questions that are suited to your class or group. Some questions ask about story facts, but others require the students to analyze story events. Higher-level questions may bring a variety of answers; ask students to justify their response with examples from the story to support their point.

- When and where was Gertrude Ederle born?
- What did her family call her? What did everyone else call her?
- What was it like to be a women in 1906?
- Why did Trudy's father tie a rope to her waist and put her into a river?
- What did Trudy discover about being in the water?
- Identify at least three of Trudy's early swimming accomplishments.
- Why would the newspapers of the time call Gertrude "courageous" and "determined"?
- How many men had successfully made the cross-Channel swim when Trudy decided to try?
- What did Trudy's trainer do on her first attempt to swim the Channel? Describe how you think Trudy may have felt.
- Why do you think Trudy decided to try the cross-Channel swim again?

- Describe at least three things that happened during the second Channel swim.

- Why did Trudy's trainer tell her to come out of the water during the second Channel swim? What was Trudy's response?

- How did the people in England guide Trudy to shore?

- How long did it take Trudy to swim the English Channel? What record did she set?

- Describe what happened to Trudy when she returned to the United States?

- What did Trudy's accomplishment demonstrate to the world?

- Describe what you think might have happened if Trudy had given up after her first failed attempt to swim across the Channel.

Character Exercises

Hold a class discussion identifying Trudy's goal and the steps she went through to accomplish it. Using the goal setting worksheet that follows this section, allow students to select a goal they would like to accomplish. Students then list steps they will need to take to accomplish the goal. You may want to do this more than once. Allow students to select an immediate goal, such as learning to play a game or ride a bike, and a long-term goal such as Trudy's goal from the story (students might select a possible career, athletic or artistic accomplishment, etc.). Have them list steps to accomplish their goal choices; be sure the steps are in proper sequence.

Provide opportunities for the students to experience situations that require perseverance in the classroom. Activities such as jigsaw puzzles, growing plants, creating or building models, and putting on a short play involve students in activities that require effort and take time to accomplish. Be sure to include opportunities during the activity for students to reflect on their feelings and experiences. Journal entries might reflect on wanting to quit or the satisfaction of accomplishment when the project is finished.

Integrate Your Curriculum

Language Arts

- Explain acrostic poetry to the students and direct them to create their own poem using the phrase "Don't Give up" using the worksheet that accompanies this chapter.

- Possible journal entries include the following:

    - A goal I worked hard to accomplish

    - A time I didn't give up

    - Why it is important to keep trying when you don't succeed?

Social Studies

- Using a globe and maps locate these places from the story: New York; Paris; Cape Gris-Nez, France; and Kingsdown, England.

- Research President Calvin Coolidge, who is mentioned near the end of the story. Identify important facts about his presidency.

- Research the Olympics, particularly focusing on the 1924 Paris Olympics in which Gertrude Ederle participated. List the athletic competitions; were women able to compete in all events? Compare the Paris games with the most recent Olympics, listing similarities and differences. Discuss what the changes in the games might tell us about the world, our country, athletics, and society.

Math

• Calculate the average miles per hour for Trudy's swim.

Ask parents to fill in the goal-setting chart, identifying a goal they set for themselves in their lives and listing the steps they had to take to accomplish the goal. Parents should then share their goal-setting chart with their child and hold a family discussion about perseverance and working to achieve your goals.

Galegroup. *Gertrude Ederle.* Available: http://www.google.com/search?hl=en&ie=UTF-8&oe=UTF-8&q=%22gertrude+ederle%22&btnG=Google+Search.

Grawberg, Melissa. *A Look at Gertrude Ederle.* Available: http://www.msu.edu/~grawbur1/iahweb.html. This site includes pictures.

Smithsonian Legacies. Silver trophy awarded to Gertrude Ederle, the first woman to swim the English Channel, in 1926. Available: http://www.smithsonianlegacies.si.edu/objectdescription.cfm?ID=99.

America's Champion Swimmer:
Gertrude Ederle
Acrostic Poem Worksheet

Directions: Acrostics are a special type of
poetry. In an acrostic poem, the letters of a word or phrase start each line in
the poem. Read the sample acrostic poem below, then create your own acrostic
poem about perseverance on the back of this sheet using the phrase "Don't
give up."

Personal best—nothing less!

Excel each day!

Really learn from my mistakes.

Strive for excellence in all things.

Expect to succeed.

Very self-disciplined.

Eliminate time wasters.

Regard failure as a challenge.

Always set goals.

Never give up when things are hard.

Careful to stay focused.

Evaluate and revise goals as needed.

GOAL

Goal-Setting Chart: Pick a goal you want to accomplish. Then list five steps you will take to accomplish your goal.

My goal is: _____

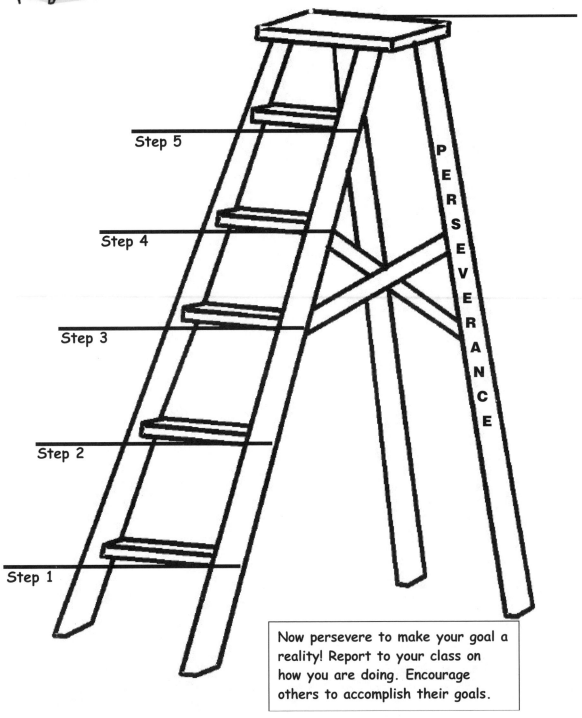

Step 5

Step 4

Step 3

PERSEVERANCE

Step 2

Step 1

Now persevere to make your goal a reality! Report to your class on how you are doing. Encourage others to accomplish their goals.

Rocks in His Head by Carol Otis Hurst

So my father took the job as night janitor at the museum.
Before he went home, he'd open some of the mineral cases and scrub
some of the rocks with a toothbrush until they sparkled like diamonds.

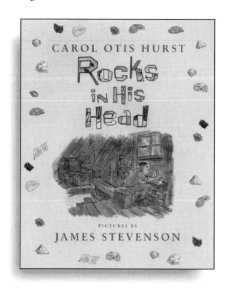

Hurst, Carol Otis. *Rocks in His Head*. Illustrated by James Stevenson. New York: Greenwillow Books, 2001. ISBN 0-06-029404-3.

Reading Level: 2.6

Interest Level: K–3 (Higher if tied in thematically with instruction)

The Story

Rocks in His Head is based on the author's father, a man who, from childhood, had an obsession for collecting rocks. He traded and displayed his collection despite the discouraging comments frequently received from family and friends. Even the hard times of the Depression did not curtail his obsession. A frequent visitor to the local science museum, he drew the attention of the museum's curator, who realized that a man with rocks in his head might be just what the museum needed!

Character Connections

Rocks in His Head is a story of perseverance. It is not the same sort of goal-oriented perseverance exhibited by Gertrude Ederle in *America's Champion Swimmer*. The hero of *Rocks in His Head* has no specific goal. Through difficult times, he perseveres by staying true to himself and his family. At the same time, he never gives up his love for rocks. It didn't matter to him that there was no money to be earned through this interest or that people said he had rocks in his head. He kept working even when his business failed and the family moved into a less than desirable house. He looked for work wherever he could find it and fixed up the house. The father in this story exhibits a calm, quiet perseverance that is heroic. He could easily have abandoned his family or refused to work as a janitor because it was beneath him. He does not do this, however, and it is his determination that ultimately leads him to the job of his dreams. Use *Rocks in His Head* to help children learn that in life we must persevere through difficult times for our friends, families, and, most important, for ourselves.

About the Author

A former teacher and school librarian, Carol Hurst is a nationally known storyteller, language arts consultant, columnist, and author. Hurst was a columnist for *Teaching K8 Magazine* for many years. She has conducted workshops on children's literature and language arts in every state in the United States as well as in many other countries. In addition to her sixteen professional books for teachers, Hurst has written five books for children: a picture book titled *Rocks in His Head* with illustrations by James Stevenson (Greenwillow) and three novels for Grades 4–6: *Through the Lock* (Houghton Mifflin), *In Plain Sight, The Wrong One,* and *A Killing in Plymouth Colony.* Her Web site (http://carolhurst.com) is an award-winning resource of information in the field of children's literature. Carol is the mother of two daughters, the grandmother of two grandsons, and lives in Westfield, Massachusetts.

About the Illustrator

James Stevenson began his life in New York City in 1929. He began writing and drawing at an early age, encouraged by his father, a watercolorist. Stevenson began his career working as a satirist and cartoonist. His work for children quickly followed, and he has written and illustrated more than two dozen books for children. In addition to his own work, he has illustrated the work of more than a dozen writers including Anna Quindlen, Dr. Seuss, and Cynthia Rylant.

Objectives

After reading this book, students will be able to

- Define related vocabulary.
- Demonstrate understanding of the story by answering related questions.
- Explain in their own words what perseverance means and how they demonstrate it in their lives.
- Identify someone who exhibits perseverance. Explain how and why their choice demonstrates this character trait.

Classroom Exercises

Prereading Activity

Locate several rock samples of various types. Pass the rocks around so that all the students can see and touch them. Be sure to identify and discuss the rocks. Note where they came from, unique characteristics, and how they formed. Ask students if they have ever seen an interesting or valuable rock. Ask if they collect or know anyone who collects rocks. Introduce and read the book.

Vocabulary

Students may need help defining the following terms. Define the terms either before reading the story or, using context clues while reading, after you have finished.

collect	chess	museum
collection	Depression	Packard
filling station	stock market	attic
Henry Ford	mineral	mineralogist

Comprehension and Values Questions

Select and use only those questions that are suited to your class or group. Some questions ask about story facts, but others require the students to analyze story events. Higher-level questions may bring a variety of answers; ask students to justify their response with examples from the story to support their point.

- Who is this story about?
- What does he collect? How long has he been collecting?
- What did the man in the story decide to do when he grew up?
- Where does this story take place?
- What was the name of the filling station?
- What was inside the filling station?
- What is a Model T?
- Where did some of the narrator's father's rocks come from?
- Why did bad times come?
- Where did the man go on rainy days when he could find no work? Why did he go there?
- Who was Grace Johnson?
- What kind of job did Mrs. Johnson offer the author's father?
- Why do you think she could not offer him a job as a mineralogist?
- What might have happened if the father in this story refused to accept the night janitor's job?
- What lessons can we learn from this story?

Character Exercises

Try this fun variation of musical chairs to help student get the idea of perseverance against difficult odds. Set up the chairs as though you are going to play traditional musical chairs. Before starting, explain to the students that this time the object of the game is not to leave anyone out. If everyone has a place to sit, the whole group wins. If someone is left out, the whole group loses. Start the game and eliminate one chair, but not a child, each time the music stops. Students will have to work together creatively to figure out ways to find space for everyone on the diminishing number of chairs.

Afterward, discuss the experience. Did it get harder to find a way to keep everyone involved? Did anyone want to give up? How did it make students feel to know that if they gave up, the whole group would lose the game? What kept students from giving up? Explain perseverance and how it applies to the game they just completed.

To relate this experience to life and the story, you might ask if there is anything in students' lives that they do even though it is difficult. Help students to understand that there are many things in their lives that require them to persevere. Students need to see this character trait as important in their day-to-day lives. To end this lesson, ask students to fill in the Perseverance Award at the end of this section.

Integrate Your Curriculum

Language Arts

- Ask students to make a list of situations that require them to demonstrate perseverance. Students might list things such as doing homework and chores or paying attention in school. Discuss the lists, then assign a paragraph or short essay about the item that requires students to demonstrate the most perseverance. In their writing, they can explain the item, why it is so difficult for them, and how they demonstrate perseverance to accomplish it.

- Brainstorm a class list of people who demonstrate perseverance. This list could include historical figures, literary characters, or people they know. After you have compiled the list, ask students to write about one person on the list, explaining how they demonstrate qualities of perseverance.

Science

- This book is the perfect accompaniment to a unit on rocks and minerals. The illustrations show several types of rocks and minerals. Assign students to study them and report to the class about the characteristics, uses, and sources of each.

- Arrange a field trip to a local science museum to study minerals.

- Invite a rock collector to come speak with the class and bring parts of his or her collection for show and tell.

Social Studies

- Locate Springfield, Massachusetts, on a map. Write the city Chamber of Commerce for more information about the town and its Science Museum.

- Study the Great Depression. Identify when it took place, who was affected by it, and how people coped with the bad times it brought.

- Study collecting and start a class collection. The book mentions several things people collect. Brainstorm with the students to create a longer list. Investigate reasons people collect things, such as economic necessity, pleasure, curiosity, social status, preservation, and so on. Select something the class can collect. It could be anything from rocks to toys or books. Assign students various tasks to set up and maintain the collection. At the end of the year, donate the collection to an appropriate charity; for example, a collection of sports cards could be donated to the children at a local homeless shelter.

Careers

- *Rocks in His Head* presents a great opportunity to have students do career research. If the story's hero had known about careers that involved his interests, he might have found success earlier in his life. Ask students to select one or two things they really like to do. They can then research possible careers that involve these things. For younger students, this might mean simply creating a list of possible careers. Older students might write a report or do a presentation for the class.

PARENTZONE: TAKING THE LESSON HOME

Send a second copy of the *Showing Perseverance* worksheet home with instructions for the children and parents to fill it out together. Ask them to select a family member or someone they know personally for the subject. Students can present their papers to the class in the form of a brief oral report. Be sure to point out that many people have to persevere through problems in their lives.

TEACHSOURCE: RESOURCES FOR TEACHERS

Bureau of Labor Statistics. *Teacher's Guide to BLS Career Information*. Available: http://stats.bls. gov/k12/html/edu_tch.htm. Refer to this before directing students to the site listed in KidSource section.

Rector, Kathy. *Rock Classification*. Available: http://chesterfield.k12.va.us/Resources/Lessons/ Rocks/lesson.html. An online lesson plan created for fourth-grade science by an elementary school teacher.

KIDSOURCE: RESOURCES FOR STUDENTS

Bureau of Labor Statistics. *BLS Career Information: Archivist and Curators*. Available: http://stats. bls.gov/k12/html/mus_004.htm.

Rocks and Minerals Slide Show. Available: http://volcano.und.nodak.edu/vwdocs/vwlessons/lessons/ Slideshow/Slideindex.html.

Perseverance means _____

_____

_____

_____

I demonstrate perseverance when I _____

_____

Explain why this shows perseverance in the space below.

_____

_____

_____

_____

Draw a picture of your act of perseverance in the box below.

Tops in
Perseverance

Showing Perseverance

On the line below, write the name of someone who demonstrates perseverance.

_____

Explain how this person demonstrates perseverance in the space below.

_____

_____

_____

_____

_____

Paste a picture of your persevering person in the box on the left. Draw a picture representing his or her act of perseverance in the box at right.

6

Respect for
Self and Others

*Every human being, of whatever origin,
of whatever station, deserves respect.
We must each respect others even as we respect ourselves.*

U Thant (1909–1974)
Secretary-General of the United Nations, 1961–1971

Respect is a cornerstone character trait. If we do not respect ourselves, we will be unhappy victims all our lives. If we do not respect others, we will have constant difficulties as we seek to move through society. These two aspects of respect go hand in hand. If we do not respect ourselves, we have no standard by which to respect others. Respecting the rights and property of others often helps us to define the way we wish to be treated. Unfortunately, teaching respect is not as easy as teaching children The Golden Rule. Like many character traits, the concept of respect takes time for children to absorb, define, and integrate into their lives. The two titles presented here will help students do this. *Hey, Little Ant* teaches about respect for others through its focus on peer pressure and the idea that might does not make right. *Smoky Night* involves respect through its focus of tolerance of others as we reach across racial and ethnic divides. In both of these stories, students are challenged to define respect for themselves as they think about how they would act in the situations presented. They will also gain an understanding of what it means to respect others, as they understand how they would want to be treated.

Hey, Little Ant by Phillip Hoose and Hannah Hoose

I can see you're big and strong,
Decide for yourself what's right and wrong,
If you were me and I were you,
*What would **you** want **me** to do?*

Hoose, Phillip, and Hannah Hoose. *Hey, Little Ant*. Illustrations by Debbie Tilley. Berkeley, CA: Tricycle Press, 1998. ISBN 1-883672-54-6.

Reading Level: 2.5

Interest Level: K–3 (Higher if tied in thematically with instruction)

The Story

Does might make right? That is the essential question behind this lighthearted poetic tale. A boy spies an ant crawling in a sidewalk crack. Should he squish the ant or not? The boy and his friends think so; the ant's point of view is decidedly different. In the end, the choice is left up to the reader and leaves open many possibilities for classroom interaction. Given its themes and open-ended approach, it is no surprise that *Hey, Little Ant* was a 1999 Jane Adams Peace Association Honor Book.

Character Connections

Respect for others is the key component of this picture book. Additional character elements include compassion and empathy. The boy's initial thought to step on the ant shows no regard for its life. After learning about the ant's family and life, the additional element of peer pressure is introduced. Finally, the ant turns the tables on the boy, asking what he would want the ant to do if the situation were reversed. This is a key element for class discussion as students are left to create their own ending to the story.

Students should not have trouble picking out the concepts and questions raised by the text; at the same time, they will need critical thinking skills to reflect on both sides of the situation because of the dual perspectives presented. Use this story to focus on respecting others. It provides a great opportunity to demonstrate and discuss how we gain and demonstrate respect in our daily lives. The advantages of respectful behavior can also be brought into the discussion, increasing student awareness of this important character trait.

About the Authors

Phillip Hoose and Hannah Hoose are a father-daughter team who wrote a song titled *Hey, Little Ant* when Hannah was nine years old. The song was recorded and became popular, which led to the publication of the book in 1998. Phillip has written five books and works for The Nature Conservancy, protecting habitats of endangered species. At the time of this writing, Hannah is a teenager and a practicing actress, dancer, and keyboardist. The Hoose family lives in Maine.

About the Illustrator

Debbie Tilley lives in Southern California and has illustrated several books for children, including *Dinosaur Dinner*, *Oops*, and *Riddleicious, Riddleightful*. She received a Society of Illustrators Award for her work on *Hey, Little Ant*. Her family includes two cats, Vinnie and Howard, and Millie the dog.

Objectives

After reading this book, students will be able to

- Demonstrate understanding of the story by answering related questions.
- Define respect and identify ideas for showing respect.
- Explain why they believe it is important to treat other people with respect.
- Demonstrate empathy with the story's characters by explaining how they feel.

Classroom Exercises

Prereading Activity

Show students the book cover. Ask them the following questions:

- What do you see in this picture?
- Who do you think is saying "Hey, little ant!"
- Why do you think the ant is on the stick?
- Do you think the person holding the stick looks happy to see the ant?
- What do you think is happening in this picture?

Comprehension and Values Questions

Select and use only those questions that are suited to your class or group. Some questions ask about story facts, but others require the students to analyze story events. Higher-level questions may bring a variety of answers; ask students to justify their response with examples from the story to support their point.

- What does the boy in the story want to do?
- What does the ant want?
- How are the boy and ant different?
- How are they alike?
- Why does the boy think that ants are bad?
- How does the ant explain taking the picnic food?
- What do the boy's friends want him to do?
- What would you want the ant to do if he was big and you were small?
- How do you think the ant feels in this story?
- What do you think happens at the end of the story and why?

Character Exercises

Before starting this activity, ask the students to think about what it means to respect someone and define respect as a class. Then ask them to think about how they think the story should end. Use the following activity to stimulate critical thinking about the stories conclusion.

This exercise encourages students to think, consider, and demonstrate their opinions. The goal of this activity is to allow students to think about the issue(s) presented and change their minds if they want to do so. Set your classroom up so that there are three groups of chairs. If there are not enough chairs, students can move them back and forth. Create a large sign that reads, "Squish the Ant" and another that reads, "Save the Ant." On a third sign, write "No Opinion." Post the signs to identify the areas. Before starting the activity, direct students to sit in the area that reflects their opinion of how the boy should act.

Ask for student volunteers to role-play the parts of the ant and the boy. Give each student a copy of the song lyrics from the back of the book. Direct the students to read their parts. Stop the action after verses two, five, eight, and nine. Each time you stop, discuss the events and information presented in the story. Survey the groups each time you stop. If students have changed their minds about what should happen, they should move to the appropriate area. You might use some of the following questions to guide your discussion:

- Why do you think the boy wants to squish the ant?
- Does the boy have a right to squish the ant?
- Does the ant have any rights?
- Should the boy be able to do anything he wants just because he is bigger?
- Do you think the boy really knows what the ant's life is like?
- Do you think the boy should consider the ant's family when he makes his decision?
- Ants are pests in many ways; why not squish the ant?
- The boy's friends think he should squish the ant, so it must be all right. Do you agree or disagree?
- Does the boy respect the ant?
- What if the situation were reversed? What if the ant were big and the boy were small. How do you think the boy would feel about the ant squishing him?

- What if this story involved two people instead of a boy and an ant? Would you feel differently? If the ant were another human being, would it be still be acceptable to squish him?

When you are done, compare the three areas. Have the numbers in each side changed? This activity provides an opportunity to point out that we do not always agree. Point out that it is important to respect everyone's opinion even if you disagree. Class members are allowed to have their own opinions and to change their minds when they consider information. Encourage everyone to treat each other respectfully even if they have different opinions. Identify ways to demonstrate respect for someone even if people disagree about something (continue to treat them fairly, continue to play with them, etc.). Brainstorm a list of respectful behaviors used each day in school. Finally, ask students to fill in the respect worksheet located at the end of this section.

Integrate Your Curriculum

Language Arts

- Possible journal topics for this story include the following:

    - In your opinion, what happens at the end of this story and why?

    - You are the voice of the boy's conscience; convince him not to step on the ant.

    - In your opinion, does the boy respect the ant? Why or why not?

Science

- Study ants! Students can identify different varieties native to your locale and other parts of the world. Identify ant anatomy. Observe and explain ant social behavior. Students will be amazed at the strength and adaptability of this small insect.

Music

- Learn the song at the end of the book. Develop simple costumes and have some students act it out as the class sings. Present it at a school program or for another class.

Social Skills

- Define and discuss peer pressure. Identify examples from the story and from the student's experiences. Role-play possible peer pressure situations and positive ways to handle them.

Send home a copy of the *We Show Respect at Home* worksheet. Ask parents to do it with their children and discuss the importance of showing respect within the family.

 **TEACHSOURCE: RESOURCES FOR TEACHERS**

10 Speed Press. http://www.tenspeed.com. Operated by the parent company of the publisher, this site contains links to book information and other related resources.

Hey, Little Ant. http://www.heylittleant.com. This is the official homepage for the story, which contains links with author information, audio of the song, lesson ideas, and more.

 **KIDSSOURCE: RESOURCES FOR STUDENTS**

Brenner, Barbara. *Thinking about Ants*. Illustrated by Barbara Brenner. Greenvale, NY: Mondo, 1997. ISBN 1-57255-210-7.

Demuth, Patricia Brennan. *Those Amazing Ants*. Illustrated by S. D. Schindler. New York: Macmillan, 1994. ISBN 0-02-728467-0.

Pascoe, Elaine. *Ants*. Nature Close-Up series. Photographed by Dwight Kuhn. Woodbridge, CT: Blackbirch Press, 1999. ISBN 1-56711-183-1.

Hey, Little Ant
Respect Worksheet

Directions: After reading and discussing Hey, Little Ant with your class, fill in your answers to the questions below.

1. What does respect mean? _____

_____

_____

_____

2. How do you show respect? List three ideas for showing respect at school.
    1. _____

    2. _____

    3. _____

3. Why is it important to treat other people with respect?

_____

_____

_____

_____

_____

 Use the back of this paper if you need more space for your answers.

Hey, Little Ant
<u>Building Empathy Worksheet</u>

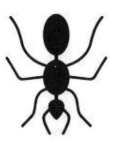

Empathy is the ability to put yourself in another person's place. It is an important tool for building respect between people. Empathy involves three things:
1. Identify how the other person feels.
2. Consider the person's point of view.
3. Express your empathy by saying something like, "I think you are feeling _____, is that correct?"
Feeling empathy will not always change your point of view on a problem, but it will help you understand and communicate with others when problems arise. The improved communication will help you to be a good, and fair, problem solver.
Sharpen your empathy skills in the space below by putting yourself in the place of the boy and the ant. Think about how each character feels about the problem he faces and write about his feelings in the space below. If you need more space, use the back of this paper.

Should he squish the ant? I believe the boy feels_____

_____

_____

_____

_____

Don't squish me! I believe the ant feels _____

_____

_____

_____

_____

Hey, Little Ant
We Show Respect at Home

Talk about and respond to the situations below. Think about your family's level of respect for each other. Circle your response to each question. Talk about why respect is important in family life.

We listen to each other.

        Always   Sometimes   Improvement Needed

We take care of our health.

        Always   Sometimes   Improvement Needed

We speak politely to each other.

        Always   Sometimes   Improvement Needed

We follow family rules.

        Always   Sometimes   Improvement Needed

We ask before borrowing.

        Always   Sometimes   Improvement Needed

We return things promptly and in good shape.

        Always   Sometimes   Improvement Needed

We treat each other fairly at all times.

        Always   Sometimes   Improvement Needed

We care about each other's feelings.

        Always   Sometimes   Improvement Needed

Smoky Night by Eve Bunting

*My mama and I don't go in Mrs. Kim's market even though it's close.
Mama says it's better if we buy from our own people.*

Bunting, Eve. *Smoky Night*. Illustrated by David Diaz.
New York: Harcourt Brace, 1994. ISBN 0-15-269954-6.

Reading Level: 2.4

Interest Level: K–3 (Higher if tied in thematically
with instruction)

The Story

In the street below their window, a riot is taking place. Daniel and his mother watch as looters break into stores and steal merchandise. Later when there is a fire in their building, they flee to a shelter. During the course of events, Daniel is separated from his pet cat. It's only when he and the cat are reunited that he learns a valuable lesson about reaching out to all kinds of people.

Character Connections

Smoky Night is rich in potential character studies. Anger, fear, prejudice, and courage are just a few of the elements present in this story. Focusing on the uncontrolled anger and prejudice creates an opportunity to focus on the importance of respect for self and others as a character trait. Share *Smoky Night* with this in mind: people who respect themselves and others do not riot and loot. They are open to people of other cultures and ethnic groups. People who respect themselves and others understand the importance of tolerance in any community, and they work to ensure it is a driving force in the world.

About the Author

Eve Bunting became a writer later in her life and has written more than 100 books for children and young adults. Born in Ireland, she immigrated to the United States with her husband and three children in 1958. She is perhaps best known for her socially conscious books like *Smoky Night*, but she writes in a variety of genres such as science fiction, romance, and nonfiction. She was inspired to write *Smoky Night* after the Los Angeles riots in 1992 caused her to wonder how children experienced the rioting.

About the Illustrator

David Diaz won the Caldecott Medal in 1995 for his work on *Smoky Night*. The book's illustrations combine textured collage backgrounds and acrylic paintings. The combined images enhance the story by providing not only a sense of time and place but a reality that simple illustrations alone could not provide. When the reader sees breakfast cereal spilled across the page it is easy to imagine Daniel watching as the food spills onto the street during the rioting. In selecting his color palette for the characters in the story, Diaz deliberately chose not to identify the ethnic background of the characters. He wished to let their personalities speak for themselves.

Objectives

After reading this book, students will be able to

- Recognize similarities and differences between themselves and their classmates.

- Explain in their own words why learning about our unique traits and characteristics can be beneficial.

- Explain anger and how it can positively and negatively affect them.

Classroom Exercises

Prereading Activity

Ask students to respond to the following statements or questions. They can answer collectively in a class discussion or individually on their own paper. Be prepared for a variety of answers and points of view. Ask students for positive suggestions for handling anger or to identify positive behavior strategies to use when dealing with people who are different from themselves.

- I think it is OK to break something when I am angry.

- We should not do business with someone who looks different from us.

- If everyone is doing something, then it must be OK.

Introduce the story by explaining that *Smoky Night* is a story about a night of uncontrolled anger in a city where people did not respect each other's differences. Ask them to listen carefully and be prepared to discuss the story's events when you are done reading.

Vocabulary

Students may need help defining the following terms. Define the terms either before reading the story or, using context clues while reading, after you have finished.

riot, rioting	fashion
angry	hooligan
appliance	shelter
steal	cot

Comprehension and Values Questions

Some of these questions ask factual information about the story, but others require students to analyze the story events. Be prepared for a variety of answers when students have to explain why something is or how they feel about something.

- What is going on outside of Daniel's apartment building? How are the people behaving? Do you think it is right or wrong? Why?

- Mama tells Daniel that people riot when they get angry. Can you imagine what might make people so angry that they would not care about what is right or wrong? How do you handle it when you become angry?

- What is the name of Daniel's cat?

- Why is the sky smoky in the story?

- Why don't Daniel and his mother shop at Kim's Market? Do you think that is right or wrong? Why?

- Why do you think Mama has Daniel sleep with his clothes on?

- Why is it hard for Daniel to go to sleep? How do you think Daniel feels?

- Why does Mama wake Daniel up in the night and what happens to them?

- Who is missing when Daniel and his mother leave the building?

- Describe the shelter. Where is it located? What is it like inside?

- What color is Mrs. Kim's cat?

- Where did the firefighter find Jasmine? What does the firefighter say the cats were doing when he found them?

- What lesson do the two cats teach Daniel, his mother, Mrs. Kim, and the others?

Character Exercises

Create a class tolerance quilt. You will need six-inch, square pieces of multicolored construction paper and a large piece of butcher paper on which to mount the squares.

Give each student a paper square to decorate. Squares can be decorated to reflect the student's home country, state, city, or town by including something representative of the place such as a flag, famous landmark, or a word or phrase in the language of the region. An alternative is to have students decorate the squares to represent themselves in some fashion. For example, they might draw a family picture, a hobby, or something that represents a club to which they belong. When the squares are done, arrange them on the banner paper and glue them down to form a quilt. Glitter pens or puff paints can be used around the edges and ends to add decoration the quilt. When it is completed, display the quilt on a wall or bulletin board. Help students understand the symbolism of the quilt, which is made up of many small pieces that are stronger when united. Be sure to draw the parallel of this to living in diverse communities where we must get along and respect each other.

As an additional exercise to help build community and respect in your class, try this exercise designed to demonstrate that we have things in common with other people. Pair up students with someone else in the class and have them make a list of their similarities and differences using the *Smoky Night* Building Tolerance worksheet at the end of this section. Point out that Mrs. Kim and Daniel's family both had cats and lived in the same neighborhood as a starting point. Challenge students to come up with at least five things they share in common with each other and five ways in which they are unique. Conclude by having the students draw a joint picture of themselves, doing something together based on one of the things on their list.

Finally, the starting point of this story comes from uncontrolled anger. Everyone gets angry but not everyone deals with his or her anger in a positive way. Part of being a responsible and respected person includes dealing with our anger in appropriate ways. People who learn how to channel their anger positively have a higher sense of self-respect and integrity. To help students understand the emotion of anger have them finish some of the following sentences.

When I get angry, I . . .

The thing that makes me the most angry is . . .

When someone is angry with me, I . . .

Discuss with students their reactions to anger. Next, have students brainstorm both good and bad ways to express their anger by creating an anger web. Discuss how people should react to anger and angry behavior. It is important to help students understand that feeling anger is normal; it is how we react to the anger we feel that makes the difference. Teach students the following acronym to conclude the lesson:

Angry acts

Never

Get or

Earn

Respect

Integrate Your Curriculum

Art

- Have students create a collage picture to illustrate some event from their own life.

Language Arts

- Possible journal topics:
    - Why is it good to learn about the differences among people?
    - Recognizing similarities between people is good because . . .

Science

- Study fire. What causes it? How does a fire burn? Are there good uses for fire?
- Study fire safety. Invite local fire officials to teach students the steps to take in case of a fire.

- Daniel says that drinking milk is not good for cats. Why? Study cats. Students could learn about different breeds, anatomy, care and feeding, natural instincts, and so on of these common household pets.

Social Studies

- Although it is not clear in the book, Mrs. Kim is probably of Asian heritage. Most American towns and cities now contain people from many parts of the world. Contact your local city government to locate census information for your area. Use a world map and have students locate the many parts of the world that are represented in your community. If possible invite speakers from different cultures to talk with students about their homelands and culture.

- The Los Angeles riots of 1992 inspired Eve Bunting to write *Smoky Night*. Study the riots. Challenge students to understand their cause, events that took place during the riots, and what changes (if any) came about because of the events.

PARENTZONE:
TAKING THE LESSON HOME

Ask parents to direct each family member to create an "Alike-Different" list for each person in the family. This list will identify one way the person listed is like the list maker and one way the other person is different. Family members should discuss their lists with each other and conclude by offering an appreciative remark to each other celebrating each individual's unique qualities.

TEACHSOURCE:
RESOURCES FOR TEACHERS

Discussion Archive: Smoky Night by Eve Bunting. Available: http://www.dalton.org/libraries/fairrosa/disc/smoky_night.html.

Educational Paperback Association. *Eve Bunting.* http://www.edupaperback.org/authorbios/Bunting_Eve.html.

Eve Bunting: Teacher Resource File. Available: http://falcon.jmu.edu?~ramseyil/bunting.htm.

Herrera, Kay, and Mathew Kampilly. *Smoky Night Anticipation Guide.* KidReach: The Online Reading Center. http://www.westga.edu/~kidreach/smoky.html.

**KidSource:
Resources for Students**

Johnston, Marianne. *Let's Talk about Being Afraid.* The Let's Talk about Library. Center City, MN: Hazelden, 1998. ISBN 1-56838-223-5.

Kids Health for Kids. *Defining Diversity, Prejudice and Respect.* Available: http://kidshealth.org/ kid/grow/tough_topics/diversity.html.

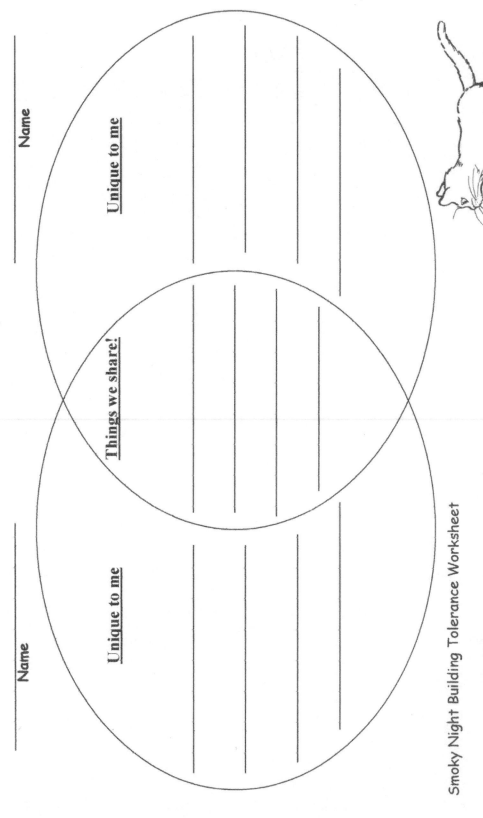

Name _____

Unique to me

Things we share!

Unique to me

Name _____

Smoky Night Building Tolerance Worksheet

Directions: Knowledge is power in the war against intolerance! Work with a partner to identify four things that are unique to each of you and four things you have in common. Be prepared to share your findings with the class.

Smoky Night
Puzzle Worksheet

Directions: See how many of the words from the list below you can find in the puzzle. Circle or highlight the words you find.

```
E  V  E  B  U  N  T  I  N  G  A  G  X  B  H
I  I  Z  L  Q  D  H  O  O  L  I  G  A  N  Z
B  F  U  E  A  N  G  R  Y  F  A  C  A  H  S
D  A  V  I  D  D  I  A  Z  U  I  M  S  M  N
L  S  I  N  E  C  N  A  I  L  P  P  A  M  I
G  H  O  A  Q  T  Y  S  T  E  A  L  R  M  E
T  I  A  D  K  L  K  E  N  M  M  S  E  P  G
O  O  Z  O  U  L  O  I  K  L  K  M  T  J  B
C  N  I  R  N  A  M  E  R  I  F  H  L  G  A
I  W  N  R  A  S  S  Y  M  J  D  Y  E  B  L
M  C  E  Y  A  O  Q  P  I  K  V  T  H  A  N
H  E  H  J  A  C  N  N  A  L  V  F  S  M  O
```

Angry	Fashion	Riot
Appliance	Fireman	Shelter
Cot	Hooligan	Smoky Night
Daniel	Jasmine	Steal
David Diaz	Mama	
Eve Bunting	Mrs Kim	

7

Responsibility and Commitment

Character—the willingness to accept responsibility for one's own life—is the source from which self-respect springs.

Joan Didion (1934–)
Slouching Towards Bethlehem

Like many character traits responsibility and commitment go hand in hand. It takes commitment to be a responsible person, and responsible people are committed to what they do and who they are. The two stories in this section present a realistic picture of responsibility and commitment by showing what happens when we behave less than ideally. Naomi, the young Amish girl in *Just Plain Fancy,* is very responsible; she fails in one important area, however. Because of her longing for something fancy, she does not tell her parents about the mysterious egg she finds and the bird that emerges. This one small slip in her otherwise responsible and honest behavior causes her to experience stress and fear as the story progresses. *Snail Started It!* demonstrates the results of one irresponsible and insensitive remark. Fortunately, both stories end well as the characters take responsibility for their actions and learn that they can overcome their mistakes. Children need to learn this, too. Mature, well-rounded people take responsibility for their actions—even when they make mistakes. Their commitment to themselves and good character demands they make things right, even if it means an embarrassing admission of guilt. These books provide a great opportunity to talk about the nature of responsibility and commitment in the classroom.

Just Plain Fancy by Patricia Polacco

"We'll have to hide him until we know what to do,"
Naomi said finally. The elders will be here for the frolic tomorrow.
"He'll be shunned," Ruth whimpered. "Maybe we will be too!"
They put Fancy into another part of the henhouse and locked the door.

Polacco, Patricia. *Just Plain Fancy*. New York:
Bantam Doubleday Dell, 1990. ISBN 0-553-07062-2.

Reading Level: 3.8

Interest Level: K–3 (Higher if tied in thematically
with instruction)

The Story

Two Amish farm girls, Naomi and Ruth, discover an egg in the grass on their farm and place it in a nest to hatch. They enjoy their exotic looking find and the unusually beautiful bird that comes from the hatched egg. Because he is so different from their plain world, the girls name the bird Fancy. When the girls learn about their community's custom of shunning, they become concerned about their feathered friend. Could Fancy be shunned because he is different? The girls hide Fancy when the community holds a frolic at their house, but he escapes and flies into the middle of the gathering. In horror the girls watch as Fancy, a beautiful peacock, spreads his tail feathers, revealing himself to all. Fancy is not shunned by the community as Naomi and Ruth feared; instead, he is embraced as one of God's most beautiful creatures.

Character Connections

Naomi is a very real character who displays several interesting character traits. She is less than honest with her family about Fancy, yet when her pet is finally out in the open at the frolic, she immediately admits that he is her responsibility. She also displays respect in many instances. Her careful handling of the egg and caretaking of the chickens indicates a respect for animals and the earth. Her concern about

Fancy being shunned shows awareness of and respect for the bird, her heritage, and the community's traditions. Naomi's is a very human character, who, despite her flaws, clearly displays responsible behavior. *Just Plain Fancy* provides teachers with a great opportunity to discuss this important character trait.

About the Author and Illustrator

In almost every book she writes and illustrates, Patricia Polacco features a young person interacting with an elderly person. This is because she had strong relationships with both sets of her grandparents. In fact, she feels that these relationships had a strong influence on her life and work. Born in 1944, Patricia's parents divorced when she was three and both parents returned to live with their parents. Whether she was with her mother or father, she was always with grandparents. Telling stories was an important part of life in each household. Patricia did not have a television set while growing up, and so she learned to rely on her imagination and listen to the inner creative voice that she believes each of us possess.

Patricia did not do well in school. At the age of fourteen, it was discovered that she had dyslexia. With help, she was able to understand how she learned information and quickly caught up with her peers. She majored in fine art in college and went on to earn a master's degree and a doctorate in art history. For a time, she worked restoring ancient art for museum collections. She wrote her first children's book when she was forty-one years old and has been writing and illustrating for children ever since.

Objectives

After reading this book, students will be able to

- Define related vocabulary.
- Demonstrate understanding of the story by answering related questions.
- Define responsibility and demonstrate responsible behavior.
- Reliably participate in classroom and school responsibility activities.

Classroom Exercises

Prereading Activity

As a group, brainstorm a list of activities students have done during the day. Encourage a specific list so that it includes things such as turning on the lights, watching TV, or listening to the radio. Ask students if they have ever heard of the Amish and brainstorm a second list of things they already know about the Amish. If necessary, be prepared to spend some time providing basic background information to set up the story. Before starting, ask students to be sure to listen closely for ways that their lives are similar to and different from the lives of the two girls in the story.

Vocabulary

Students may need help defining the following terms. Define the terms either before reading the story or, using context clues while reading, after you have finished.

Amish	fancy	shun (shunned)
buggy	white cap	ordnung
English	working bee	botherment
henhouse	frolic	pleasure (pleasured)
responsibility	down feathers	peacock
plain	washhouse	miracle

Comprehension and Values Questions

Select and use only those questions that are suited to your class or group. Some questions ask about story facts, but others require the students to analyze story events. Higher-level questions may bring a variety of answers; ask students to justify their response with examples from the story to support their point.

- How are Kaleb, Naomi, and Ruth traveling at the start of the story? Why do they choose to travel this way?
- What is Naomi's responsibility? What does she have to do to take care of the chickens?
- What does Naomi mean when she says, "Everything here is so plain"? Give some examples of some of the plain things in Naomi's world.
- What did Naomi want to have? Why do you think she wanted something fancy?
- What did Naomi and Ruth find in the tall grass? Why did they decide to put the egg in Henny's nest?
- What do you think it means for Naomi to get her white cap?
- What did Naomi name the chick that hatched from the fancy egg?
- Why did the woman from the neighboring community have to be shunned?
- Why did Ruth and Naomi learn that it was wrong to be fancy?
- What does it mean to shun someone? How is it done?
- How did Naomi feel after she learned about shunning? Why did she feel this way?
- Why do the girls hide Fancy?
- Name some activities the men and women did at the working bee or frolic.
- What happened when Fancy escaped from the henhouse?
- According to Martha, Fancy will not be shunned. Why?
- What does Martha give Naomi? How has Naomi earned this reward?
- What do you think Naomi learned that day at the frolic?

Character Exercises

Ask students to fill in the What Would Happen If . . . worksheet at the end of this section. While they are working, enlist a few students to role-play one of the situations on the worksheet. For example, set up a trash can overflowing with trash. You play the role of the school custodian who decides not to empty the trash. Allow a student or students to try to convince you to do your job. While they are trying to convince you, other students can add to the growing trash pile. This fun, improvised skit will drive home the point about responsibility in a memorable way.

Based on the What Would Happen If . . . exercise, ask students to explain why behaving responsibly is important. Define responsibility. On the chalkboard, list ways Naomi showed responsibility in the story. In a second column, list ways people demonstrate responsibility at school. Answers might include things such as teachers planning lessons or students doing their homework. End by having students complete the Responsibility Pledge worksheet at the end of this section.

Follow up this lesson by creating a classroom care list. This list should include things that need to be done daily or weekly to keep the class environment running smoothly. Items on the list might include picking up trash, sharpening pencils, sorting books or paper, cleaning desktops, and so on. Assign students to these chores and make them a part of your normal routine. The tasks can be reassigned periodically so that students can share in all the assignments.

Finally, brainstorm a class responsibility project. This project will be something your class agrees to do for the school on a regular basis to demonstrate responsible behavior. The whole class or a small group might do it as long as everyone participates over time. Project ideas will vary depending on your school needs but might include peer tutoring a lower grade level class, adopting an area of the campus to keep clean, escorting new students on orientation tours, or helping in the school library or media center.

Be sure to recognize students periodically throughout the year for their responsible behavior and participation in the classroom and school projects.

Integrate Your Curriculum

Art

- Draw a picture of the Vlecke's farm or something that depicts Naomi and Ruth's life.

- Draw a picture of Fancy or use brightly colored tissue or construction paper to create a collage of Fancy. Students can draw, color, and cut out the main body of the bird. Then create colorful tail feathers using the tissue or construction paper and glue. Paste the bird body over the top of the feathers to create a two-dimensional effect.

- Younger students might use a tracing of their hands to create a peacock drawing. Their thumb becomes the birds head, and remaining fingers are the colorful tail feathers.

Science

- Study peafowl. What is their native habitat? What do they eat? How long do they live? How do male and female birds differ? Learn about the male bird's distinctive call. When an egg is laid, how long does it incubate? How long does it take a chick to mature into an adult bird? If possible, visit a zoo to see peafowl or locate a local breeder who will bring a bird for the students to see and who can answer questions about this beautiful animal.

Social Studies

- Study the Amish in the United States. Where did they come from? Get a map and locate Amish communities around the country. Learn about their customs. How are Amish children educated? What do they wear? How do they live? How are their lives similar to the lives of the students in your class, and how are they different? If possible bring in some examples of Amish food (recipes are available on the Internet), quilts, and other artifacts for students to see and share. Students could create Venn diagrams comparing and contrasting their lives with the lives of the Amish.

Language Arts

- Examine the story for its setting. How does Patricia Polacco convince the audience that they are in a real Amish community?

- Discuss symbolism. The white cap clearly indicates something about Naomi and can help students understand this concept and her character. Be sure to ask students which privileges they might earn as Naomi earned the privilege of wearing her white cap.

- The author uses onomatopoeia at the start of the story. Discuss this literary device and ask the students to brainstorm other examples.

PARENTZONE: TAKING THE LESSON HOME

Send home the Family Responsibility Pledge sheet located at the end of this section. Ask students and parents to fill it in together listing things they will be responsible for at home. Stress the importance of parents participating in this activity with their children so that students realize the many responsibilities shouldered by the adults in their lives.

TEACHSOURCE: RESOURCES FOR TEACHERS

The Amish: Not to Be Modern. Video. 57 Minutes. MPI Home Video, 1988.

Amish Heartland Magazine. Available: http://www.amish-heartland.com/magazine.htm. Be sure to read the about the Amish page.

Just Plain Fancy: A Day in the Live of the Amish. Available: http://www.wiu.edu/users/mfeam/Amish%20Life.htm.

Patricia Polacco.com. Available: http://www.patriciapolacco.com. Note: this is a wonderful Web site featuring downloadable artwork, including pictures and other information about *Just Plain Fancy* and other books by Patricia Polacco.

Wells, Deborah. *Just Plain Fancy by Patricia Polacco.* Available: http://www.sru.edu/depts/scc/elem/fancy.htm.

KidsSource:
Resources For Students

The Amish, the Mennonites and the Plain People: The Amish Frequently Asked Questions. Available: http://www.800padutch.com/atafaq.shtml.

Bial, Raymond. *Amish Home.* Boston: Houghton Mifflin, 1993. ISBN 0-395-59504-5.

Coleman, Bill. *Amish Photo Gallery.* Available: http://www.amishphoto.com/galleryindex.htm.

Israel, Fred L. *Meet the Amish.* The Peoples of North America series. New York: Chelsea House, 1986. ISBN 0-87754-853-6.

Photograph of peacock at the National Zoo in Washington, D.C. Available: http://washingtondcmetroweb.com/peacock.htm.

WNC Nature Center. *Animal Facts: Indian Peafowl.* Available: http://wildwnc.org/af/peafowl.html.

Yolen, Jane. *Raising Yoder's Barn.* Illustrated by Bernie Fuchs. New York: Little, Brown and Company, 1998. ISBN 0-316-96887-0.

What Would Happen If . . .

Imagine what would happen in the situations below. Write your thoughts in the space provided.

What would happen if

the crossing guard did not tell me when it is safe to cross the street?

_____

_____

the librarian decided not to check in the books?

_____

_____

the custodian decided not to clean up the school?

_____

_____

the teacher decided not to teach?

_____

_____

the cafeteria workers decided not to cook one day?

_____

_____

When these people come to school and do their jobs, how are they behaving?

_____

Just Plain Fancy
Responsibility Pledge

In the space below, list five ways you will show responsibility at school. Sign your name at the bottom to show your commitment to this pledge.

<u>Example:</u> Doing my homework and bringing it back to school each day.

I will show responsibility at school by
1. _____

_____

2. _____

_____

3. _____

_____

4. _____

_____

5. _____

_____

Name_____

Date:_____

Just Plain Fancy
Family Responsibility Pledge

List five ways you will show responsibility at home in the space below. Sign your name at the bottom to show your commitment to this pledge.

I will show family responsibility by

Student	Parent
Example: by helping clean up after meals.	Example: by taking my child to school each day.
1.	
2.	
3.	
4.	
5.	

Signed: _____   Signed: _____

Date: _____   Date: _____

Snail Started It! by Katja Reider

*One day Snail met a pig. "My you are fat!" said the snail.
"I'm surprised your legs don't give way under all that weight!"*

Reider, Katja. *Snail Started It!* Illustrations by Angela von Roehl. Translated by Rosemary Lanning. New York: North-South Books, 1997. ISBN: 1-55858-706-3.

Reading Level: 2.8

Interest Level: K–3 (Higher if tied in thematically with instruction)

The Story

This chain reaction story is set in motion when Snail meets Pig and remarks, "My you are fat!" Even though Pig declares she is happy with herself, she takes the remark to heart and when she meets Rabbit, she insults him. Rabbit in turn insults Dog and so on until it gets back to Snail. Sulking in his shell, Snail remembers what he said to Pig and realizes the error of his ways. Apologies follow and all the animals are able to return to their normal happy lives.

Character Connections

Snail Started It! provides a great opportunity to discuss with students the power of words. Even if Snail's remark was unintentional, it was hurtful and caused Pig to doubt herself. The chain reaction of insults seems to have sprung from anger and provides an opportunity to discuss motive with students. Children need to realize that many times we unknowingly take out our frustrations on others around us instead of thinking about and dealing with our feelings.

The strongest feature of this story however is the realization on the part of Snail that his remark to Pig was unkind and his willingness to do something about it—apologize! Taking responsibility for our actions and seeking to correct our mistakes are important traits of persons with strong character.

About the Author

Katja Reider was born in 1960 in Goslar, Germany. She currently lives in Hamburg with her husband and two children. She worked as a freelance publicist specializing in youth and environmental issues before beginning her writing career.

About the Illustrator

Angela von Roehl studied illustration and graphic design in London and Hamburg. She runs a studio that develops interactive projects for museums as well as art books.

Objectives

After reading this book, students will be able to

- Define related vocabulary.
- Demonstrate understanding of the story by answering related questions.
- Explain why speaking in anger is not a positive action.
- Identify positive ways to handle their anger.

Classroom Exercises

Prereading Activity

Ask students if they can define the word *insult*. Once you have a definition, ask them to think about a time when they may have been insulted and ask them how it made them feel. Ask how they handled the situation. Point out to the students that often when we are insulted, we tend to take our anger out on someone else. Ask them to listen to the story you are about to share and pay attention to how the characters deal with their anger.

Vocabulary

Students may need help defining the following terms. Define the terms either before reading the story or, using context clues while reading, after you have finished.

reflection	spindly legs	sulk
dainty	annoy (annoyed)	indignant
timid	coward (cowardly)	apologize
scold	molehill	insult
lazy	chat	

Comprehension and Values Questions

Select and use only those questions that are suited to your class or group. Some questions ask about story facts, but others require the students to analyze story events. Higher-level questions may bring a variety of answers; ask students to justify their response with examples from the story to support their point.

- What did Snail say that insulted Pig?
- Why do you think Snail made this comment to Pig?
- How did Pig respond to Snail's insult?

- What happened after Pig had time to think about Snail's remark?
- Why do you think Pig insulted Rabbit?
- Why does Dog say he has a good life?
- What happened when Dog was upset?
- Why did Spider say Goose should not be so calm?
- What did Snail find so enjoyable about his day climbing the molehill?
- How did Goose insult Snail?
- What did Snail realize as he sat sulking in his shell?
- What did Snail do after he realized he had insulted Pig?
- What if Snail had not apologized to Pig? How might things have been different?
- What happens because of Snail's apology?

Character Exercises

For this exercise, set up a few tabletops with paper protective covers. You will need enough paper plates and small travel-sized toothpaste tubes for your class when divided into small groups.

Divide the students into small groups of three or four students. Give each group a toothpaste tube and paper plate. Direct the students to pretend they are mad at something or someone. Holding the toothpaste tube over the paper plate, each student should squeeze a line of toothpaste on the plate while saying a pretend mean comment. After students have squeezed the tube, direct them to return the toothpaste to the tube. Of course, this is not possible. The point of this exercise is that harsh words, like the toothpaste, cannot be taken back. Ensure that students understand this.

Brainstorm positive ways to handle anger. Examples might include to stop and count to ten, to breathe deeply, to walk away and talk with someone you can trust, and so on. When you are done, ask students to fill in the Handling Your Anger worksheet at the end of this chapter. Finally, discuss the importance of taking responsibility for your angry words. Discuss the advantages of apologizing when you have said or done something wrong. For fun, direct the students to return to their small groups and challenge them to list different ways to say I'm sorry. This exercise might also help review dictionary and thesaurus use. Make it into a small contest providing prizes for the teams with the most answers.

Integrate Your Curriculum

Art

- After studying the animals in the story, ask students to select one and draw their own picture of it in its natural habitat. Make a bulletin board display of the pictures and research reports.

Language Arts

- Possible journal topics include the following:
  - Tell about a time you were insulted. What happened? How did it make you feel? How did you react to the person who insulted you? Thinking back, did you react the right way? Could you have reacted differently? How might a different reaction have been better?
  - Tell about a time you insulted someone. Why did you make the remark? How did the person you insulted react? If you could go back in time, how would you handle the situation differently?
  - How is responsibility shown in this story? What are some other ways a person can demonstrate responsibility. Why is it important to take responsibility for your actions?

Science

- Study the various animals and creatures in the story. What are their main characteristics? Do they possess the qualities mentioned in the story?

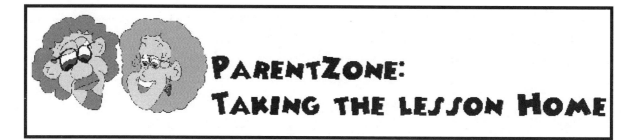

Use the Watching for Anger worksheet at the end of this chapter, ask parents and their children to watch a television program together looking for examples of anger. Parents and children should discuss how the television show might affect people. Encourage them to discuss the example set by characters in the show and compare the show with real-life situations in which anger might arise.

American Psychological Association. *Controlling Anger Before It Controls You.* Available: http://www.apa.org/pubinfo/anger.html.

Begun, Ruth Weltman, compiler. *Ready-to-Use Social Skills Lessons & Activities for Grades 4–6.* West Nyack, NY: Center for Applied Research in Education, 1996. ISBN 0-87628-865-4.

Johnston, Marianne. *Dealing with Anger.* The Conflict Resolution Library. New York: Rosen Publishing/PowerKids Press, 1996. ISBN 0-8239-2325-8.

KidsHealth Resources for Kids. *Saying You're Sorry.* Available: http://www.kidshealth.org/kid/feeling/home_family/sorry.html.

Simon, Norma. *I Was So Mad!* Illustrated by Dora Leder. Morton Grove, IL: Albert Whitman, 1974. ISBN 0-8075-3519-2.

Snail Started It!
Handling Your Anger

In the story, Snail did not handle his anger
well, causing many hurt feelings. Brainstorm
with your class, and then list five positive
ways to handle your anger in the spaces below.

1. _____

_____

2. _____

_____

3. _____

_____

4. _____

_____

5. _____

_____

Remember, angry words hurt!
Once you've said them,
you cannot take them back!

Snail Started It!
Watching for Anger

Directions: Select a television show to watch as a family. Watch for angry behavior in the show. The angry behavior may be mild or extreme. Answer the following questions about what you watched.

1. In the space below, write the name of the television program you watched.

_____

2. Tally the number of angry episodes you saw in the program.

Mildly angry:　　　　　　　**Angry:**　　　　　　　**Strong violent anger:**

_____

3. Do you think the characters handled their anger well? Why or why not?

_____

_____

_____

4. Do you think watching anger on television affects people? Why or why not?

_____

_____

_____

To talk about with your family:
In real life, how would you have handled the angry situations you saw?
Talk about and share some of the reasons it is hard to control your anger.
Talk about and share positive ways to handle anger.

8

Self-Control

By constant self-discipline and self-control,
you can develop greatness of character.

Grenville Kleiser (1868–1953)

Without self-control, our lives would be chaos. We exercise this character trait daily in all of our activities. Self-control is easy when we enjoy what we are doing and the people involved. When the situation is difficult or the people involved are not pleasant, however, self-control becomes more challenging. Ironically, it is these difficult times when practicing self-control is usually the most important. In extreme cases, our very survival could depend on our ability to think and control our actions. The story *Baseball Saved Us* presents such a situation. A Japanese American family and community uprooted during World War II is forced to move to an internment camp. The stress-filled living situations cause a breakdown in family culture as anger and resentment builds throughout the group. The seemingly simple solution of bringing baseball to the camp provides a lesson for everyone—especially the storyteller, who learns he can control his emotions and succeed through difficult circumstances. Even though their situations are not as dramatic as those experienced by the families in *Baseball Saved Us,* students will relate to many aspects of the young storyteller's experiences and learn the importance of taking control of their lives and emotions to succeed.

Baseball Saved Us by Ken Mochizuki

We stared at each other. Then I blocked out the noise around me and got set. The pitcher wound up and threw.

Mochizuki, Ken. *Baseball Saved Us*. Illustrated by Dom Lee. New York: Lee & Low Books, 1993. ISBN 0-880000-19-9.

Reading Level: 3.9

Interest Level: 4–6 (Higher if tied in thematically with instruction)

The Story

This compelling picture book tells the story of a group of Japanese Americans being held in an internment camp during World War II. Surrounded by fences, guards, and harsh desert, the people face daily humiliation and injustice. Narrated by a young boy living in the camp, the story picks up when the boy's father decides the people need something to do and begins designing a baseball field. Gradually the entire camp joins in, building the field and organizing teams. The sport gives them a sense of purpose and accomplishment. More than just giving them something to do, it helps return a small amount of dignity to the people's lives.

The narrator recounts his experiences playing in the camp, always under the watchful eyes of the guards. Returning home after the war, he continues to face prejudice and hatred. Yet when baseball season returns, the other children notice his improved play immediately. Summoning his inner strength, the narrator does not give up. Instead, he perseveres and wins for his team—and himself.

Character Connections

The people in this story are under great stress. They also demonstrate incredible perseverance and patience. They are courageous, inventive, and filled with initiative. Be sure to point out these things as you work with students reading the story. It is the self-control, however, that characters such as the boy and his father exhibit that shines brightest in *Baseball Saved Us*. Imagine how different the lives of the people would have been if the father had given up on his baseball idea or used his anger in a negative way. By maintaining his self-control, he provided for his family and community. He also modeled for his son a valuable lesson that would pay off in the end.

About the Author

Ken Mochizuki's parents were in the Minidoka internment camp during World War II, giving him a family connection to the experiences of his characters in *Baseball Saved Us*. His inspiration for the story, however, came from an article about a first generation Japanese American who built a baseball diamond and formed a league within the camps. Mochizuki is a novelist, journalist, and actor. He is a native of Seattle, Washington, and a graduate of the University of Washington.

About the Illustrator

A native of South Korea, Dom Lee received his bachelor's degree in fine arts from Seoul National University and his master's degree from the School of Visual Arts in New York. He and his wife currently live in New Jersey. The photographs of Ansel Adams inspired some of his illustrations for this book.

Objectives

After reading this book, students will be able to

- Identify stressful situations.
- Define self-control.
- List positive ways to handle stressful situations.
- Identify a stressful event from their life and explain how they handled the situation in a way that demonstrated self-control.

Classroom Exercises

Prereading Activity

Read the quote from *Baseball Saved Us* that starts this chapter to the students. Hiding the title, show them the book cover. Ask them to write a sentence explaining what they think the story is about and a prediction sentence about the story. Be sure to refer back to these statements when you are done to see how many were correct.

For an additional prereading activity, see the directions for making cereal necklaces in the character exercises section of this section. Without explaining the purpose, give students their cereal necklace to wear before you start with the story. Simply instruct them not to damage their necklaces. After the story has been read, see if anyone has eaten any of his or her cereal pieces. Use this as a means to discuss the story's theme of overcoming stress with positive self-control.

Vocabulary

Students may need help defining the following terms. Define the terms either before reading the story or, using context clues while reading, after you have finished.

desert

barbed wire

Japan, Japanese, Japanese American

Pearl Harbor

barracks

Comprehension and Values Questions

Select and use only those questions that are suited to your class or group. Some questions ask about story facts, but others require the students to analyze story events. Higher-level questions may bring a variety of answers; ask students to justify their response with examples from the story to support their point.

- Why is Shorty's family in the camp?
- Why did Shorty's parents come to get him out of school?
- Describe the people's life in the camp.
- Why were people upset when Teddy talked back to his father?
- Did the people have the things they needed for starting the baseball teams? How did they get what they needed?
- When Shorty came up to bat, what did the other teams usually think?
- What caused Shorty to hit a home run in the championship game at the camp?
- Describe Shorty's life after the war when he returned home.
- How did Shorty feel at the game when he realized no one looked like him?
- Why did Shorty think about pretending he was sick so that he would not have to take his turn at bat?
- At the end of the story, when Shorty went up to bat, what did the pitcher remind him of? How do you think it made Shorty feel?
- What happened when Shorty hit the ball?
- Imagine what would have happened in this story if Shorty's father had not pursued his idea of playing baseball. What would have happened to the people in the camp?
- Imagine what would have happened to Shorty if he had pretended to be sick during the game at the end of the story. How would his life have been different?

Character Exercises

Exercise 1 Stress Chart Worksheet. Use a dictionary to define stress and then identify stressful situations in the story using the *Baseball Saved Us* stress chart worksheet. Brainstorm a list of situations that cause stress for your students. For each item on your list, ask students to suggest a positive way to handle the situation.

Compare the positive ideas for handling stressful situations. Look for common threads that tie them together. Common positive reactions to stress include the following:

- Stop to think about the stressful situation. Decide what has upset you and why.
- Try to remain calm while counting to ten.
- Think, don't just react, about what you will do next, which could include discussing your feelings with the person(s) involved, leaving the situation, speaking with a neutral person, recording your

feelings in a journal, and brainstorming and discussing possible positive solutions for everyone involved.

Identify these techniques and others from the positive responses generated by the students. Once you have identified them, use them as examples of practicing self-control. Create a class definition for self-control based on your examples.

Finally, use the self-control reaction sheet from this section to allow students to identify a personal stressful situation, the effect it had on them, and how they feel about it now.

Exercise 2. To reinforce the concept of self-control, try the following exercise with your students.

You will need strands of yarn or string about eighteen to twenty-four inches long, a dough-nut-shaped cereal such as Fruit Loops (use something colorful and sweet that students will want to eat).

Make cereal necklaces with the yarn by stringing it through the holes in the cereal. Give one to all students and challenge them not to eat the cereal. Make it a game by providing a small prize for the student with the most cereal on his or her necklace at the end of a predetermined period of time.

A variation on this exercise for older students is to associate certain cereal colors with different feelings or emotions. Responding angrily to a situation might cause a student to lose a green cereal ring for example.

Be sure to discuss student reaction to the exercise when finished. Identify elements of self-control that students displayed and relate life in a broader sense.

Integrate Your Curriculum

Art

- Using a large, colorful piece of butcher paper, create a banner for the classroom. In large letters, write "I will practice self-control when under stress." Then list the positive ways to handle stress identified by your class. Have students decorate the edges of the banner with handprints using various colors of nontoxic craft paint. Signatures can be added by their handprints with crayons or markers. Fix the banner on a wooden dowel and attach colorful curled ribbon streamers for additional decoration. Display the banner in the classroom to create a lasting visual reminder of the lesson for the students.

Language Arts

- Ask students to identify a time in their own lives when they had to summon up enough courage and self-control not to run away from something. Challenge them to write a journal entry explaining the event, how they felt, why they did not run away, and how they felt afterward. Students could also approach this from the opposite perspective writing about a time they did not stand up for themselves and how their choice affected them.

Science and Math

- Baseball is a game of statistics. Teach students how to average a player's runs per game or season to help reinforce addition and division skills.

- Research the actual size of a baseball diamond. To practice measuring skills, take students out to the playground or other area and measure out a regulation ball field.

- The camp in the story is in a desert region. Study desert environments focusing on plant and animal life, weather conditions, and so on.

Social Studies

- Study World War II identifying important dates and events. Create a timeline to display in the classroom.

- Baseball is called America's game. Study this uniquely American sport; identify important events in the history of baseball and investigate the status of the sport today.

Urge parents to hold a dialogue with their children about stress, sharing examples of stressful times and how they handled the situation. It is important for students to understand that adults feel stress too and often struggle with handling it correctly. Suggest that the family agree on a code word to signal that a stressful situation exists for one or more members of the family. Then the family should agree on possible positive ways to react to the person(s) experiencing the stress (leaving them alone for a few minutes, asking how to help, etc.).

If possible, have a class field day. Invite parents to participate and include a friendly game of baseball with everyone (adults and children) playing. Use the game as an opportunity to teach good sportsmanship by having the teams shake hands before and after the game in a gesture of mutual support.

**TeachSource:
Resources for Teachers**

Children of the Camps. A PBS documentary, for information and an online teacher's guide see http://www.pbs.org/childofcamp. This documentary is not for small children. It is best used to provide the instructor background information and insight.

Japanese American Internment Camps during World War II. Available: http://www.lib.utah.edu/spc/photo/9066/9066.htm. This site contains photographs from the special collections department of the J. Willard Marriott Library, University of Utah, and Private Collections. The photos are of the Topaz camp in Utah and the Tule Lake camp in northern California.

National Baseball Hall of Fame and Museum. The official homepage for the hall of fame located in Cooperstown, New York. Available: http://www.baseballhalloffame.org/.

**KIDJJOURCE:
REJOURCEJ FOR JTUDENTJ**

Note: The resources listed below came from the PBS Web site Rabbit on the Moon. Available: http://www.pbs.org/pov/pov1999/rabbitinthemoon/resources/index.html. Booklist compiled the recommended children's books. Additional titles are available on the Web site. The site also lists adult resources as well.

Recommended for Elementary Grades

Uchida, Yoshiko. *The Bracelet*. New York: Putnam/Philomel Books, 1993.

Uchida, Yoshiko. *Journey Home*. New York: Aladdin Books, 1992.

Recommended for Middle Grades

Savin, Marcia. *The Moon Bridge*. New York: Scholastic, 1995.

Stanley, Jerry. *I Am an American: A True Story of Japanese Internment*. New York: Crown, 1996.

Uchida, Yoshiko. *The Invisible Thread: An Autobiography*. New York: William Morrow, 1995.

Baseball Saved Us
Self-Control Reaction Sheet

<u>Directions:</u> Use this sheet to think about sources of stress. Imagine different negative and positive ways to react to your stress. Discuss with your teacher and class why your positive self-controlled reaction is better. On the back of this paper, write a paragraph explaining in your own words why you should always try to use self-control.

Stress Situation	Negative Response (Lacks control)	Positive Response (Shows self-control)
Example: You accidentally trip while walking to the teacher's desk to turn in your paper. Someone laughs at you.	Become angry and yell at the person who laughed.	Take a deep breath and count to ten to relax. Realize everyone trips from time to time. Decide to ignore the laughter.
You tried your very best on a school project, but the teacher still asks you to do more.		
Your friend asks you to come play video games, but you have homework to do.		
(Imagine your own stress situation in this square.)		

Baseball Saved Us
Stress Chart

Shorty and his family experienced a lot of stress in the story. Identify a source of stress experienced by each of the following characters in the story. Then tell how they handled the stressful situation.

Character	Source of Stress	Stress Response
Example character: Dad	Forced to give up his home and move his family to the camp.	Realized the people needed something positive to do and started the baseball teams.
Shorty		
Teddy (Shorty's brother)		

Self-control is the ability to handle the stressful situations in our lives in a positive manner. It means that even though you may feel angry, very sad, or hurt, you recognize that you need to concentrate on something more important.

Which character in the chart did not show self-control? How might he have handled his stress in a more positive manner? Write your answers in the space below:

_____

_____

_____

_____

9

Sharing

Happiness is not so much in having as sharing.
We make a living by what we get,
but we make a life by what we give.

Norman MacEwan

The ability to share is an important part of American culture. True, we respect personal ownership, but we also admire and hold in high esteem those who are willing to give away some or all of what they have. As a nation, we have a history of sharing our resources with each other and the world. In our states and communities, we do the same. The ability of the individual to share is also important. Sharing demonstrates our understanding and compassion for others. It takes us out of our isolation and involves us with the lives and feelings of others. Sharing builds our self-respect and our respectability. The two stories presented here involve sharing on different levels. *Don't Need Friends* shows how a simple act of sharing can help break down the walls we build around ourselves. *The Gift* profiles the selfless sharing of a young girl born out of love for her mother. Reading these stories will help students understand the importance of sharing for the people they choose to share with and for themselves.

Don't Need Friends by Carolyn Crimi

Rat had a best friend named Possum. Rat and Possum did everything together until Possum had to move to another junkyard, leaving Rat behind. So one fall day Rat made a decision. "Don't need friends, don't need 'em at all," he grumbled.

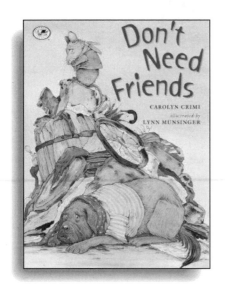

Crimi, Carolyn. *Don't Need Friends*. Illustrated by Lynn Munsinger. New York: Random House, 1999. ISBN 0-385-32643-2.

Reading Level: 5.5

Interest Level: K–3 (Higher if tied in thematically with instruction)

The Story

Feeling hurt and lonely after his best friend Possum moves away, Rat decides he does not need friends. Rejecting the other animals in the junkyard, Rat leads a lonely life. Time passes and a grouchy dog moves into their neighborhood. Dog and Rat quickly become enemies, growling and grumbling at each other all day. Rat does start to notice things about Dog, however, and wonders why Dog howls at the moon each night. One day Dog gets sick and does not growl at Rat. He stays in his barrel all day sniffling and sneezing. When Rat finds a foot-long salami sandwich, he faces a choice. Should he share his tasty find with his enemy?

Character Connections

Don't Need Friends points to the need for compassion, sharing, and friendship in our lives. When Rat will not share with the other animals or allow them to share with him, he cuts himself off from the world and creates a lonely existence for himself. It is only when he breaks through his own barrier and shares the salami sandwich with Dog that he once again begins to enjoy his life. Sharing the sandwich demonstrates compassion and allows Rat and Dog to become friends. We need friends in our lives. Compassion and sharing are key elements in the development of any relationship. As we share time, experiences, belongings, and feelings with the people we know, our friendships deepen and grow. The ability to act with compassion increases. Our lives take on purpose and meaning beyond the needs of self, and we become better human beings capable of giving and receiving. This is the lesson Rat learns in this endearing story.

About the Author

On her Web site, Carolyn Crimi lists her occupation as "Princess"! This rising star of children's literature is indeed a princess as demonstrated by her wonderful books, including *Outside, Inside*; *Kidding around Chicago*; and *Tessa's Tip-Tapping Toes*. Crimi lives in Evanston, Illinois, with her husband, Alfonso Segreti, and a cat, Oscar Crimi-Segreti. She is a graduate of Lake Forest College and earned her master of fine arts degree in writing for children from Vermont College.

Crimi considers herself to be a lucky person because she always wanted to be a children's author. When she is not writing, she enjoys unfrosted Blueberry Pop Tarts, black-and-white monster movies, and rainy days. She also teaches adult education courses on writing for children, visits schools for author talks, and contributes to children's textbooks and magazines.

About the Illustrator

Born in Greenfield, Massachusetts, in 1951, Lynn Munsinger graduated from Tufts University in 1974. She continued her studies at the Rhode Island School of Design and received a bachelor of fine arts degree in 1977. Munsinger is the illustrator of more than eighty children's books, including *Tacky the Penguin*, *What Mommies Do Best/What Daddies Do Best*, and *The Three Blind Mice Mystery*. Munsinger is a dedicated artist whose illustrations help tell the stories created by more than twenty-five authors.

Objectives

After reading this book, students will be able to:

• Demonstrate understanding of the story by answering related questions.

• Discuss the importance of working together to solve problems and build community.

• Discuss friendship and sharing, explaining in their own words what these terms mean.

• Identify ways they can share with other students in the classroom and at home with their families.

• Identify acts of compassion and select one to do as a class.

Classroom Exercises

Prereading Activity

Ask students to identify things they enjoy doing with their friends. List some of the activities on the board. Before reading the story, ask students to imagine how they might feel if the person with whom they did these fun activities suddenly had to move away and could not spend time with them anymore. Introduce Rat by explaining that this is what happened to him and then begin the story.

Comprehension and Values Questions

Select and use only those questions that are suited to your class or group. Some questions ask about story facts, but others require the students to analyze story events. Higher-level questions may bring a variety of answers; ask students to justify their response with examples from the story to support their point.

- How did Rat feel when Possum moved away?
- How did Rat treat the other animals after Possum moved away? Can you give specific examples from the story to prove your answer?
- Why was Rat rude to the other animals? Do you think he was right to act this way? Why or why not?
- How did the other animals feel about the way Rat treated them? How did they show their feelings?
- Describe Dog.
- How were Rat and Dog alike?
- Why do you think Dog howled at the moon?
- What happened to Rat and Dog when winter came? Do you think they were happy? Why or why not?
- One day Rat noticed Dog behaving differently. How was dog behaving?
- What treasure did Rat find? Why do you think Rat decided to share his sandwich?
- What happened to Rat and Dog after they shared the sandwich? Can you give some specific examples from the story to prove your answer?
- What do you think Rat and Dog learned in this story?
- How do you think Rat felt about Possum at the end of the story?

Character Exercises

Exercise 1: Jigsaw Puzzles. Purchase a number of jigsaw puzzles appropriate to your student's age and ability. Be sure to have enough puzzles so that you can easily divide students into small groups of two to four students. Divide the pieces of the puzzles into plastic bags so that each student gets a bag with puzzle pieces. Be sure you have the students grouped at tables with the other students who have their puzzle, but don't tell them they will have to share pieces to put the puzzle together. Direct them to begin assembling their puzzle pieces. Some students may figure out that they have to share to complete the puzzle. Others may need guidance. If after a short time students are having difficulty, you can suggest they combine their bags and share pieces to see if it becomes easier to complete the puzzle.

When the puzzles are completed, hold a class discussion. Ask students if they think they would have finished the puzzles as quickly by themselves even if they had all the pieces. You might use some of the following questions as prompts for further discussion:

- How is doing this puzzle together like experiences we have in life?

- Why do we all benefit when we share?

- What happens when we share with people over and over again? How does it affect our relationship with them?

- Do you always have to have an object, like a salami sandwich, to share? Can you share unseen things? Give some examples of unseen things people share.

- Can you think of some ways you can share with other people in our classroom? At home? In our community?

Encourage students to pick one thing they will share with someone before the next class, then follow-up by asking about their experiences and feelings.

A fun variation on this exercise would be to divide the students into small groups giving them different bags containing the ingredients needed to make a foot-long salami sandwich. Eating their creation would be a fun treat and a direct tie-in to the story.

Exercise 2: Acts of Compassion. Define *compassion* and write the definition on the board. Provide examples such as, "compassion is caring about how others feel or putting other people's needs before your own." Ask students to find examples in the story that show Rat's changing attitude toward Dog. Rat's attitude change gradually leads him to an act of compassion. Ask students to identify Rat's compassionate act. Reread the last four or five pages of the story with the class then ask the students what happens as a result of Rat's single act of compassion. Student answers may vary, including factual events (Dog let Rat come into his barrel to stay warm), and broader understanding (Rat and Dog became friends). Help students realize that none of these events would have taken place had Rat not acted on his compassion for Dog.

Ask students to fill in the Acts of Compassion worksheet accompanying this section. Then share their responses as a class. Select one or two projects to do as a class. Projects might be collecting school supplies, sponsoring a clothing drive for less fortunate people, or performing a school-based community service project such as cleaning up a playground. Another possibility is for your class to adopt a senior citizen center or retirement home. Students can make cards and write letters to residents at holidays, birthdays, or other special occasions.

Integrate Your Curriculum

Art

- Ask students to draw a picture of something they share with someone special to them. Their picture might show them playing a game with a friend or sharing a meal with their family. Use the pictures as the basis for the language arts activity that follows.

- The illustrations for *Don't Need Friends* are done in watercolor paints. Allow the students to experiment with watercolors. They could first try painting on dry paper, then using a brush and clean water; lightly wet another section of the paper. When students paint on the wet section of the paper, they will notice a softer, blurry look to the paint and colors. Consult an art teacher or artist for additional watercolor techniques.

Science

- Identify the various animals in the story and create a small group project for students to study them. Each group could study one particular animal and share their findings with the class.

Language Arts

- Direct students to write a paragraph explaining their sharing picture. Combine the pictures and paragraphs to form a class book or bulletin board display.

- Help students explore compassion with the following journal prompts:

    - I showed compassion once by . . .

    - Tell about a compassionate act someone once did for you.

    - Do you think an act of compassion can change the world? Why or Why not?

    - Why is it important to be compassionate?

Ask parents to share with their children the story of how they met their best friend. Encourage them to include some of the experiences they have shared with their friend and the ways they have helped each other by sharing and being compassionate.

Ask parents and students to work together to fill out the Thinking about Friendship and Sharing worksheet included in this section. Students should return the worksheet for class discussion.

Carolyn Crimi's Web site. Available: http://www.carolyncrimi.com. The site includes biography information, background on her books, and more.

KidSSource:
Resources For Students

Pleasant Grove Elementary School, Henry County Georgia. *Friendship*. Available: http://www. henry.k12.ga.us/pges/kid-pages/friendship/default.html.

Raatma, Lucia. *Cooperation*. Character Education series. Mankato, MN: Bridgestone Books, 2000. ISBN 0-7368-0506-0.

Raatma, Lucia. *Friendliness*. Character Education series. Mankato, MN: Bridgestone Books, 2000. ISBN 0-7368-0368-8.

Don't Need Friends
Acts of Compassion Worksheet

After your class discussion about compassion, define
what it means in your own words:

Compassion is _____

_____

_____

Spend a few minutes brainstorming. In the space below, list some people you
know that need some help. Then list a helpful act of compassion you might be
able to do for them.

Person that needs help	How you can help this person
Examples: Older neighbors School Janitor Children in the hospital A friend from school	Bring their newspaper to them or help rake their yard Sweep our classroom floor and bag up the trash Hold a toy drive and deliver toys to hospital Help with homework

Finally, fill in the statement below to show how you will act compassionately today!

I will demonstrate compassion today by helping _____ with

_____ .

I Do Need Friends!

Draw a picture in the space below of something you like to do with one of your friends.

My picture shows my friend _____ and I. We are

Don't Need Friends
Thinking about Friendship and Sharing

After reading the story and talking with your class,
write your thoughts about friendship and sharing in the
spaces below. Be ready to share your ideas with the
rest of the class!

Friendship is:

_____
_____
_____
_____
_____
_____
_____

What is sharing?

_____
_____
_____
_____
_____
_____
_____
_____

Important friendship
qualities are:

_____
_____
_____
_____

Things I can share:
    With my friends

_____

    With my class

_____

    With my family

_____

    With my community

_____

The Gift by Marcia S. Freeman

I thought of Mama. I touched the lace and ribbons one more time,
then put them back on the shelf.

Freeman, Marcia S. *The Gift*. Illustrated by Patrice Kennedy. Gainesville, FL: Maupin House, 2002. ISBN 0-929895-51-7.

Reading Level: 2.5

Interest Level: 4–7 (Higher if tied in thematically with instruction)

The Story

Moving to the United States from Norway, Sonia and her father are comforted along the way by her mother's singing. Mama's singing buoys the family's spirits on the ship as they cross the ocean. Her melodies provide a background as they cross the country in a covered wagon and build their new home out of sod bricks. As winter approaches, however, Mama's voice quiets and then stops. Her spirits are not raised the following spring when a letter bearing sad news arrives from Norway. After a second hard winter, Sonia and her father travel into town to buy supplies. On the trip, Sonia takes mittens she knitted over the long winter. She hopes to sell them and then use her mitten money to buy a treat, but when it comes time to make her purchase, what should she buy?

Sonia's unselfish decision to use her mitten money to purchase a gift for her mother ultimately brings a happy ending to this wonderful story and sets the stage for a classroom lesson on the value of sharing.

Character Connections

There are many positive character traits in *The Gift*. Creative teachers can use it to teach traditional American values such as independence, self-initiative, and responsibility to family. It is Sonia's decision to share or give up her mitten money to buy the bird for her mother, however, that makes the story compelling. Sonia's decision is a huge act of love and sacrifice for a child. Sonia shares all she has to buy the bird for her mother. Use *The Gift* to teach students about the joy that can be gained from choosing to share with their friends, families, and community.

About the Author

The Gift is Marcia S. Freeman's first picture book. The author of several chapter books for children including *Catfish and Spaghetti* and *Prairie Light,* her children's books often reflect her childhood experiences, including hearing family stories, selling blueberries, and exploring the woods in rural Vermont where she grew up. Freeman attended a one-room schoolhouse as a schoolgirl. She graduated from Cornell University and also writes primary science books and professional books for educators.

About the Illustrator

Patrice Kennedy received her bachelor of fine arts degree from the Ringling School of Art and Design, where she is currently an instructor. She lives in Sarasota, Florida, with her husband, Joe, and is currently working on writing and illustrating her own children's books.

Objectives

After reading this book, students will be able to

- Define sharing in their own words.
- Identify a time when someone shared with them.
- Identify a time when they shared with someone else.
- Identify positive results from sharing for both the person who shares and the person who receives the sharing.
- Participate in a service activity to promote sharing in the school or community.

Classroom Exercises

Prereading Activity

Place maps on the walls or bulletin boards. Provide globes and atlases for students to study. Help them locate Norway and the Northern Plains states of America.

Hold a class discussion using the following prompts to stimulate discussion:

- If you lived in Norway and wanted to move to America, how would you get here?
- What if you lived over a hundred years ago before airplanes, how would you travel to America?

- Why do you think someone would choose to leave his or her homeland and move to America?

- What do you think life is like for people who live in the Northern Plains states today?

- What might it have been like for early settlers when they moved there more than a hundred years ago?

Have the children draw a picture showing some aspect of the discussion—how they think early settlers may have come to America or traveled to the northern plains or lived once they got there.

Vocabulary

Students may need help defining the following terms. Define the terms either before reading the story or, using context clues while reading, after you have finished.

oxen	dandelion
loam	melody
parsnips	warble (warbly)
blizzard	

Comprehension and Values Questions

Select and use only those questions that are suited to your class or group. Some questions ask about story facts, but others require the students to analyze story events. Higher-level questions may bring a variety of answers; ask students to justify their response with examples from the story to support their point.

- How did Sonia's family come to America?

- How did they travel to their new land?

- Why do you think Mama's singing helped the family as they traveled?

- How did Papa build the family's new home?

- Why did the family keep a garden?

- Why did Sonia play with dollies instead of real friends? How do you think Sonia felt about not having real friends?

- What is knitting?

- Where did Sonia's family come from?

- Why do you think Mama stopped singing?

- Why did Mama knit each night?

- Why could Aunt Anika and Uncle Fredrik not come to America? How did Mama feel when she heard this news?

- What did Mama do to show she was sad?

- Why did Papa bring the animals into the house?

- Why did Sonia and Papa go into town when spring came?

- What did Sonia plan to do with her mittens?

- Name some things Sonia might have bought with her mitten money.

- What did Sonia decide to do with her mitten money?

- Why do you think Sonia decided to buy the bird for her mother?

- Why did Mr. Flynn say the bird was not worth buying?

- What did Mama name the canary?

- What happened with Henrik and Mama?
- Why do you think Mama and Henrik helped each other to sing?
- Describe how Sonia felt when she heard Mama sing at the end of the story.

Character Exercises

Exercise 1: Sharing in Action. This exercise could be a possible pre- or post-reading activity. Purchase several large bags of chips and bring them to class. After getting the students attention, open a bag and begin to eat the chips in front of the students. Make a point of discussing how good the chips are and so on. Offer to give some chips to one of the students then change your mind. Draw the students into a discussion about your actions using questions such as the following:

- Is there anything wrong with what I'm doing?
- Why is it wrong?
- Why should I share my chips? I paid for them—they're mine!
- What is so good about sharing?

After the class has discussed the advantages of sharing, be sure to share the chips with everyone in the group. If you have used this as a prereading activity, read the story while the students eat their chips.

Exercise 2: Service Project. Identify a need in your school community or in the community at large and involve your class in a service project to help meet the need. Some possible project ideas might include the following:

- Make "We Care Bags" for children in a local homeless shelter. Use small brown lunch-size bags. Collect items such as pens and pencils, paperback books, stickers, crayons, bookmarks, small candies, or snack items to fill the bags. Students can decorate the bags with original artwork or seasonal designs for fun.
- Identify a need in your school community such as helping students new to the school. Students can create welcome kits to help them feel more at home. Kits might include simple items such as school supplies, a school map or directory, school spirit items, or stickers.
- Organize a food or clothing drive for a local charity.

There are many possible service projects a class can do. Students can be involved in identifying groups and needs, making decisions about the project, collecting and assembling items, and distributing the final product. The more direct student involvement there is, the more ownership students will feel in the project. They will also better understand the relationship between their actions and the fact that they are sharing their time, talents, and treasures.

Exercise 3: Sonia's Mitten Money. Bring in some of the things that Sonia might have bought with her mitten money. Discuss with what life was like for children growing up on the prairie. Help students understand that Sonia and her family had no electricity, TV, car, and so on. She probably only had one or two dresses (no pants) and almost never ate candy. It is important for students to understand Sonia's life to have a better understanding of her sacrifice. You might have students work in groups to look through some of the resources listed below about pioneer life.

Using an overhead projector or chalkboard, brainstorm a list of words describing how Sonia's mother felt (lonely, sad, etc.). Ask students to describe what Sonia did for her mother and help them to define the true nature of and reasons behind Sonia's choices. Work with the students to brainstorm a list of words describing Sonia's actions, examples might be sharing, giving, and caring.

Using the worksheets that accompany this section, direct students to list three times that they shared with someone and three times someone shared with them. They can choose one of the instances to illustrate. Hold a class discussion centered on how it feels when someone shares with you, and how it feels when you share with someone. Finally, end with the following questions: What does sharing mean to me? Why is it important to share? Have students write a brief journal entry answering both questions.

Integrate Your Curriculum

Art

- Find someone in your community who knits and ask the person to do a demonstration for the class of this traditional craft. Perhaps the person will be willing to bring in several handmade items for a display and teach a lesson or two if any students are interested in learning how to knit.

Geography and Social Studies

- Go beyond the maps to study Norway. Learn about its people, geography, and history.
- Identify and study the Northern Plains states. Learn about the history, people, and geography. Focus on the lives of children during the times of the pioneers.

Science and Math

- If your class is reading *The Gift* in winter, use the Internet, your local newspaper, or the weather channel to track the temperature in some of the major cities in the Plains states. Create a graph showing the temperatures over a week's time. Discuss how the family might have survived the harsh plains winters before electricity and heat.
- Do a report on canaries, the type of bird in the story. Where do they come from, what is their natural habitat? Perhaps someone in the class will have one for a pet, and it can be brought in for the children to see.

Language Arts

- The author uses alliteration and onomatopoeia in the text. Take time to explain these literary terms to the class. Identify examples from the text. Allow students to create their own examples of alliteration and onomatopoeia and then incorporate them into a paragraph or story.

Ask parents to share a family story that involves sharing and sacrifice with their children. The students can draw a picture to illustrate the family story and bring it in to share with the class. Make a bulletin board of the pictures and share them with the class.

TeachSource:
Resources For Teachers

American Singer's Club: The National Organization for the American Singer Canary. Available: http://www.upatsix.com/asc/index.html. This site includes information about local clubs and organizations that show canaries in competition. Check to see if there is a local group in your area.

Lewis, Barbara A. *The Kid's Guide to Service Projects: Over 500 Service Ideas for Young People Who Want to Make a Difference.* Minneapolis, MN: Free Spirit, 1995. ISBN 0-915793-82-2. An excellent resource for identifying, planning, and executing many types of service projects with students.

Maupin House: *The Gift.* Available: http://www.maupinhouse.com/book/thegift.htm. This site contains information about the book and the author and provides links to a downloadable teacher's guide.

Widgeon Weir Aviary. Available: http://www.widgeonweiraviary.com/index.htm. This site includes pictures of various canary breeds.

KidsSource:
Resources For Students

Kalman, Bobbie. *The Early Family Home.* The Early Settler Life series. New York: Crabtree, 1982. ISBN 0-86505-017-1.

Kalman, Bobbie. *Early Schools.* The Early Settler Life series. New York: Crabtree, 1982. ISBN 0-86505-015-5.

Kalman, Bobbie. *Early Settler Children.* The Early Settler Life series. New York: Crabtree, 1982. ISBN 0-86505-019-8.

Kalman, Bobbie. *Early Settler Storybook.* The Early Settler Life series. New York: Crabtree, 1992. ISBN 0-86505-021-X.

Kalman, Bobbie. *Early Stores and Markets.* The Early Settler Life series. New York: Crabtree, 1981. ISBN 0-86505-002-3.

Kalman, Bobbie. *Early Travel.* The Early Settler Life series. New York: Crabtree publishing, 1981. ISBN 0-86505-007-4.

Kalman, Bobbie. *Food for the Settler.* The Early Settler Life series. New York: Crabtree, 1982. ISBN 0-86505-013-9.

Kalman, Bobbie. *Games from Long Ago.* Historic Communities series. New York: Crabtree, 1995. ISBN 0-86505-482-7.

Kalman, Bobbie. *19th-Century Clothing.* Historic Communities series. New York: Crabtree, 1993. ISBN 0-86505-493-2.

Kalman, Bobbie, and Tammy Everts. *A Child's Day.* Historic Communities series. New York: Crabtree, 1994. ISBN 0-86505-494-0.

Kalman, Bobbie, and David Schimpky, David. *Old-Time Toys.* Historic Communities series. New York: Crabtree, 1995. ISBN 0-86505-481-9.

Teachers interested in exploring early settler life should consult with their local library for additional titles in the Historic Communities and Early Settler Life series. These books are well written, illustrated, and designed for easy student use.

Sharing Is Caring!

In *The Gift* by Marcia S. Freeman, Sonia gives up all her mitten money to buy her mother a gift. Sonia could have bought many things with her money but decided to share it by buying Henrik instead. Sonia shared because she cared about her mother. Has anyone ever shared with you? Have you ever shared with someone else?

In the spaces below, describe your experiences with sharing.

Tell about a time when someone shared with you.

_____

_____

_____

How did it make you feel to know that someone chose to share with you and why did you feel that way?

_____

_____

_____

Tell about a time when you shared with someone.

_____

_____

_____

How did you feel when you choose to share with another person? Why did you feel that way?

_____

_____

_____

Sharing
Is Caring

Sharing
Is Caring

Sharing
Is Caring

Sharing
Is Caring

Copy and distribute these bookmarks to the students as a reminder of reading *The Gift*.

Henrik Coloring Page

Bibliography

General Resources

Abourjilie, Charlie. *Developing Character for Classroom Success: Strategies to Increase Responsibility, Achievement, and Motivation in Secondary Students.* Chapel Hill, NC: Character Development Publishing, 2000. ISBN 1-892056-07-0.

Bartleby.com. *Familiar Quotations: A Collection of Passages, Phrases, and Proverbs Traced to their Sources in Ancient and Modern Literature.* Available: http://www.bartleby.com/100/. Accessed 2002–2003.

Begun, Ruth Weltman, editor. *Ready-to-Use Social Skills: Lessons & Activities for Grades 4–6.* West Nyack, NY: Center for Applied Research in Education, 1996. ISBN 0-87628-865-4.

Blair, John. *Commentary: Character Forms Essence of True Heroes.* Available: http://www.aetc.randolph.af.mil/pa/AETCNS/Oct2001/01-216.htm. Accessed March 19, 2003.

Brooks, B. David. *Young People's Lessons in Character: Teacher's Management Guide.* San Diego, CA: Young People's Press, 1996. ISBN 1-57279-025-3-4.

Creative Classroom Online. *How Would You Handle the Situation?* Available: http://www.creativeclassroom.org/jf0ttt/index3.html. Accessed March 19, 2003.

Creative Classroom Online. *Tough to Teach—Quit It!* Available: http://www.creativeclassroom.org/jf01ttt/index4.html. Accessed March 19, 2003.

Hall, Amanda. *Character Education: Ideas and Activities for the Classroom.* Greensboro, NC: Carson-Dellosa, 1998. ISBN 0-88724-456-4.

Howley, Ronda, Melissa Mangan, Katie Oplawski, and Jody Vogel. *Building Character and Community in the Classroom K–3.* Cypress, CA: Creative Teaching Press, 1997. ISBN 1-57471-294-2.

Lamme, Linda Leonard, Suzanne Lowell Krogh, and Kathy A. Yachmetz. *Literature-Based Moral Education: Children's Books and Activities for Teaching Values, Responsibility, and Good Judgment in the Elementary School.* Phoenix, AZ: Oryx Press, 1992. ISBN 0-89774-723-2.

Levy, Marc. *"We don't know why"—Pennsylvania Police Search for Motive in Deadly School Shooting.* Associated Press, April 25, 2003 (retrieved from the LexisNexis online database).

Lewis, Barbara A. *Being Your Best: Character Building for Kids 7–10.* Minneapolis, MN: Free Spirit, 2000. ISBN 1-57542-063-5.

Lewis, Barbara A. *The Kid's Guide to Service Projects: Over 500 Service Ideas for Young People Who Want to Make a Difference.* Minneapolis, MN: Free Spirit, 1995. ISBN 0-915793-82-2.

Lewis, Barbara A. *A Leader's Guide to Being Your Best: Character Building for Kids 7–10.* Minneapolis, MN: Free Spirit, 2000. ISBN 1-57542-064-3.

LibrarySpot.com. Available: http://www.libraryspot.com/. Accessed May 1, 2003.

Likona, Thomas. *10 Reasons for Character Education. Values in Action Online Newsletter,* July 1997. Available: http://www.ethicsusa.com/article.cfm?ID=178. Accessed April 25, 2003.

Logan, Claudia. "Character Education by the Book." Available at Scholastic.com: http://teacher. scholastic.com/professional/todayschild/charactered.htm. Accessed March 19, 2003.

Nish, Steven, editor. *Good Ideas to Help Young People Develop Good Character*. Marina del Rey, CA: Joseph and Edna Josephson Institute of Ethics/Character Counts, 1996–1998. ISBN 1-888689-10-2.

Novelli, Joan. *Using Caldecotts across the Curriculum*. New York: Scholastic Professional Books, 1998. ISBN 0-590-11033-0.

The Quotations Page. Available: http://www.quotationspage.com/. Accessed May 2003.

Quotes on Character, Courage and Conscience. Available: http://pages.ivillage.com/diamond2b/ home.html. Accessed March 19, 2003.

Williams, Craven E. *Character Education: Courage*. Available: http://www.gborocollege.edu/ prescorner/courage.html. Accessed March 19, 2003.

American Too

The Gale Group. *Biography Resource Center: Ted Lewin 1935–*. Contemporary Authors Online, 2001. Available: http://www.galenet.galegroup.com. Accessed January 14, 2003.

America's Champion Swimmer: Gertrude Ederle

Educational Paperback Association. *David Adler*. Available: http://www.edupaperback.org/ suthorbios/Adler_David.html. Accessed November 8, 2002.

Houghton Mifflin Reading. *Meet the Author: David A. Adler*. Available: http://www.eduplace.com/ kids/hmr/mtai/widener.html. Accessed November 8, 2002.

Houghton Mifflin Reading. *Meet the Illustrator: Terry Widener*. Available: http://www.eduplace. com/kids/hmr/mtai/widener.html. Accessed 2/4/03.

Manasse, Michele. *Terry Widener*. Available: http://www.new-work.com/twthumb.htm. Accessed 2/4/03.

Baseball Saved Us

Baseball Saved Us *Teacher's Guide*. Available: http://www.leeandlow.com/teacher/guide1.html. Accessed February 14, 2003.

The Gale Group. *Biography Resource Center: Ken Mochizuki 1954–*. Contemporary Authors On-line, 2001. Available: http://www.galenet.galegroup.com. Accessed February 14, 2003.

Houghton Mifflin Reading. *Meet the Illustrator: Dom Lee*. Available: http://www.eduplace.com/ kids/hmr/mtai/dlee.html. Accessed September 18, 2002.

Don't Need Friends

Crimi, Carolyn. *Carolyn Crimi: All about Moi* and *Don't Need Friends*. Available: http://www. carolyncrimi.com. Accessed on December 29, 2002.

De Grummond Collection, McCain Library and Archives, University Libraries, University of Southern Mississippi. *Lynn Munsinger Papers.* Available: http://avatar.lib.usm.edu/~degrum/ findaids/munsinge.htm. Accessed on December 30, 2002.

Teacher's@Random: Don't Need Friends. Available: http://www.randomhouse.com/teachers/catalog/ display.pperl?isbn=0440415322. Accessed December 29, 2002.

Enemy Pie

Author Chats.com. *Derek Munson Author Chat.* Available: http://www.authorchats.com.

Stanton, Jane. *Art Academy News, Tara Calahan King: Book Illustrator.* Available: http://www. artacademy.edu/kingLW01.htm. Accessed November 10, 2002.

The Flag We Love

Charlesbridge Publishing. *Pam Muñoz Ryan, Author* (publisher's author biography sheet). 2002.

Charlesbridge Publishing. *Ralph Masiello, Illustrator* (publisher's illustrator biography sheet). 2002.

The Gift

Freeman, Marcia S. *Teachers' Guide to The Gift.* Gainesville, FL: Maupin House, 2002.

Hey, Little Ant

The Concord Consortium/HighWired.com.

Gruener, Barbara. *Ants at Jamison?* Available: http://www.highwired.net/Guidance/Article?0, 1269,4183-31569,00.html. Accessed October 19, 2001.

Hey Little Ant Homepage. Available: http://www.heylittleant.com. Accessed October 19, 2001.

Hoose, Phillip. *A Teachers' Guide to Hey Little Ant.* Berkeley, CA: Ten Speed Press, 2001.

Literacy Review: Hey, Little Ant. Available: http://www.lane.educ.ubc.ca/courses/310/jw99/takashib/ literacy.htm. Accessed October 19, 2001.

Ten Speed Press Web site. *Hey Little Ant.* Available: http://www.tenspeed.com/catalog/tricycle/ item.php3?1d=783. Accessed October 19, 2001.

Values in Action! Comprehensive Character Education for Schools. *Family Respect Check-up.* Available: http://www.allaboutrespect.net/family_respect_check.htm. October 19, 2001.

Hooway for Wodney Wat

Brooks, B. David, and Rex K. Dalby. *The Self-Esteem Repair and Maintenance Manual.* Edited by Paula J. Hunter. Newport Beach, CA: Kincaid House, 1990. ISBN 0-943793-27-0.

The Gale Group. *Biography Resource Center: Helen Lester, 1936–.* Contemporary Authors Online, 2001. Available: http://www.galenet.galegroup.com. Accessed March 17, 2003.

Raatma, Lucia. *Courage.* Character Education series. Mankato, MN: Bridgestone Books, 2000.

Just Plain Fancy

The Heartwood Institute. *Just Plain Fancy*. Available: http://www.heartwooeethics.org/resources/libraries/bridgeBuilders.asp?a=4&s=1. Accessed December 31, 2002.

Just Plain Fancy: A Day in the Live of the Amish. Available: http://www.wiu.edu/users/mfeam/Amish%20Life.htm. Accessed December 31, 2002.

Polacco, Patricia. *Who the Heck Is Patricia Polacco?* Available: http://www.patriciapolacco.com. Accessed January 2, 2003.

Wells, Deborah. *Just Plain Fancy by Paticia Polacco*. Available: http://www.sru.edu/depts/scc/elem/fancy.htm. Accessed December 31, 2002.

Oliver Button Is a Sissy

The Gale Group. *Biography Resource Center: Thomas Anthony dePaola, 1934–*. Contemporary Authors Online, 2001. Available: http://www.galenet.galegroup.com. Accessed January 21, 2003.

Harris, Cecilia. *1658 Positive Words*. Teachers.net Lesson Bank. Available: http://www.teachers.net/lessons/posts//1658.html. Accessed January 21, 2003.

Tomie dePaola. Available: http://bingley.com/Biography.html. Accessed November 8, 2002.

Rocks in His Head

Carol Hurst's Children's Literature Site: Carol Otis Hurst's Bio. Available http://www.carolhurst.com/bios/carolbio.html. Accessed April 17, 2003.

The Gale Group. *Biography Resource Center: James Stevenson 1929–*. Contemporary Authors Online, 2001. Available: http://www.galenet.galegroup.com. Accessed January 15, 2003.

Kridler, William. *Help for "They Won't Let Me Play with Them!"* Available Scholastic.com: http://teacher.scholastic.com/professional/classmgmt/playhelp.htm. Accessed March 19, 2003.

Smoky Night

Cooperating School Districts. *RESPECT: Connections Elementary Lesson Plan*. Available: http://info.csd.org/staffdev/chared/Connections/elementary/elem.html. Accessed April 29, 2003.

The Gale Group. *Biography Resource Center: Anne Evelyn Bunting 1928–*. Contemporary Authors Online, 2001. Available: http://www.galenet.galegroup.com. Accessed February 4, 2003.

The Gale Group. *Biography Resource Center: David Diaz*. Major Authors and Illustrators for Children and Young Adults Supplement, 1998. Available: http://www.galenet.galegroup.com. Accessed February 4, 2003.

Snail Started It!

365 Ways to Share Love with Your Child. A Daily Expressions Calendar, 2003. Colorado Springs, CO: Current, 2003.

Katja Reider. Available: http://www.carlsen4teens.de/autoren/autorensuche/author.reider/. Accessed September 24, 2003.

Teaching Guide: Controlling Anger for Grades K–5. Available: http://www.goodcharacter.com/GROARK/Anger.html.

This Land Is Your Land

Jakobsen, Kathy. *About Myself.* Available: http://www.our-home.org/kathyjakobsen/myself.htm. Accessed January 3, 2003.

This Land Is Your Land: Woody Guthrie. NCAP Lesson Plan 1999. Available: http://www.siskiyous.edu/EisenhowerArts/LessonPlans/Folkart.htm. Accessed January 23, 2003.

What's So Terrible about Swallowing an Apple Seed?

All about Harriet Lerner. Available: http://www.harrietlerner.com/pages/about.html. Accessed November 9, 2002.

The Gale Group. *Biography Resource Center: Harriet Lerner 1944–.* Contemporary Authors Online, 2001. Available: http://www.galenet.galegroup.com. Accessed January 24, 2003.

HarperCollins.com. *Catharine O'Neill Author Bio.* Available: Http://www.harpercollins.com/catalog/author_xml.asp?AuthorId=12554. Accessed April 21, 2003.

Values in Action! *Family Respect Check-up.* Available: http://allaboutrespect.net/family_respect_check.htm. Accessed April 27, 2003.

Index

About the Author

CLAIRE GATRELL STEPHENS is Media Specialist, Walker Middle School, Orange County Public Schools, Orlando, Florida.